ROAD&TRACK

ON

AUBURN CORD & DUESENBERG

1952-1984

Reprinted From
Road & Track Magazine

ISBN 1 869826 469

Published By
Brooklands Books with permission of Road & Track
Printed in Hong Kong

Road & Track on Alfa Romeo 1949-1963
Road & Track on Alfa Romeo 1964-1970
Road & Track on Alfa Romeo 1971-1976
Road & Track on Alfa Romeo 1977-1984
Road & Track on Aston Martin 1962-1984
Road & Track on Auburn Cord & Duesenberg 1952-1984
Road & Track on Audi & Auto Union 1952-1980
Road & Track on Audi & Auto Union 1980-1986
Road & Track on Austin Healey 1953-1970
Road & Track on BMW Cars 1966-1974
Road & Track on BMW Cars 1975-1978
Road & Track on BMW Cars 1979-1983
Road & Track on Cobra, Shelby & Ford GT40 1962-1983
Road & Track on Corvette 1953-1967
Road & Track on Corvette 1968-1982
Road & Track on Corvette 1982-1986
Road & Track on Datsun Z 1970-1983
Road & Track on Ferrari 1950-1968
Road & Track on Ferrari 1968-1974
Road & Track on Ferrari 1975-1981
Road & Track on Ferrari 1981-1984
Road & Track on Fiat Sports Cars 1968-1987
Road & Track on Jaguar 1950-1960
Road & Track on Jaguar 1961-1968
Road & Track on Jaguar 1968-1974
Road & Track on Jaguar 1974-1982
Road & Track on Lamborghini 1964-1985
Road & Track on Lotus 1972-1983
Road & Track on Maserati 1952-1974
Road & Track on Maserati 1975-1983
Road & Track on Mercedes Sports & GT Cars 1970-1980
Road & Track on MG Sports Cars 1949-1961
Road & Track on MG Sports Cars 1962-1980
Road & Track on Mustang 1964-1977
Road & Track on Pontiac 1960-1983
Road & Track on Porsche 1951-1967
Road & Track on Porsche 1968-1971
Road & Track on Porsche 1972-1975
Road & Track on Porsche 1975-1978
Road & Track on Porsche 1979-1982
Road & Track on Porsche 1982-1985
Road & Track on Rolls Royce & Bentley 1950-1965
Road & Track on Rolls Royce & Bentley 1966-1984
Road & Track on Saab 1955-1985
Road & Track on Triumph Sports Cars 1953-1967
Road & Track on Triumph Sports Cars 1967-1974
Road & Track on Triumph Sports Cars 1974-1982
Road & Track on Volvo 1957-1974
Road & Track on Volvo 1975-1985
Road & Track on Volkswagen 1951-1968
Road & Track on Volkswagen 1968-1978
Road & Track on Volkswagen 1978-1985

Distributed By

Road & Track
1499 Monrovia,
Newport Beach,
California 92663, U.S.A.

Brooklands Book Distribution Ltd.,
Holmerise, Seven Hills Road,
Cobham, Surrey KT11 1ES,
England

Contents

We are frequently asked for copies of out of print Road Tests and other articles that have appeared in Road & Track. To satisfy this need we are producing a series of books that will include, as nearly as possible, all the important information on one make or subject for a given period.

It is our hope that these collections of articles will give an overview that will be of value to historians, restorers and potential buyers, as well as to present owners of these automobiles.

Salon
Auburn 851

I once knew a man who sprinkled sugar half an inch thick all over his steak. That was the only way he would eat it. And he insisted on wearing a Sou'wester at dinner. He also kept a beautiful supercharged Auburn in his greenhouse.

He never drove the car that anybody knew of. In fact he wouldn't even let the salesman drive it from the agency when it was new. He simply wrote out a check in full for the car and then hired a trucking company to carry it twelve miles out to his place. Then he had them pull the wheels off, and put the Auburn up on blocks in the greenhouse. I've been kicking myself ever since that I didn't get better acquainted with this gentleman. But I was a kid then and couldn't see anything different about him.

That was my first connection with what I think is the raciest looking car this country ever produced.

Auburn never built many of these unusual boat-tailed bombs. In fact I didn't see my second one for a couple of years.

I was walking down San Francisco's Market Street with a school chum (nearly 18 years ago), when the heir to a shipping fortune came grumbling around the corner in his Auburn (which must have been an identical twin to the one pictured here). I well remember how lucky I thought the driver was—he, with a shipping magnate for a father. I only had an uncle with a brewery.

So the supercharged Auburn has always had a rather special and strange place in my heart. It's no wonder that I came to a screeching halt when I spotted Bud Wittenberg's beauty in his show window . . . one night when I was cruising down Crenshaw Boulevard in Los Angeles. I had seen this particular specimen before (I found out later)—when it won a Concours d'Elegance at a recent sports car meet. I'm not surprised that it got the blue ribbon. Nobody could believe that a twenty-year-old car could be in such condition—absolutely showroom.

"What am I going to do with the car? Well, it's for sale if that's what you mean," Bud told me from his well-over six feet of blonde, lanky height, "but I've got the price set high on purpose."

Wittenberg said that he hoped nobody would buy the Auburn, but as a natur'l-born salesman by trade, he just had to put a price on it. When he heard that *Road and Track* readers would like to hear about the 851, he said, "wull . . ." Then he grinned. "But be careful of it, will you?" and he tossed over the keys.

How much do you remember about this car—which came out in 1935? Probably, if you're like me, you're only concerned with the way it handled and looked, but we may as well kick a few superficial facts around in here before we take it on the road . . . things like a centrifugal supercharger, driven by the timing gear chain and speeded up to 5.75 times crankshaft speed by use of a unique friction-planetary gear arrangement . . . which raised the horsepower output to 150 at 4000 rpm . . . eight cylinders . . . bore and stroke: 3 1/16 x 4¾, with a 6.5:1 compression ratio (7.1 optional) . . . side valve engine. The displacement was 279.9 cubic inches, in both the supercharged and unsupercharged versions . . . the latter putting out 35 hp less.

I don't know what kind of psychology motivated all of us back in those mid-depres-

sion years, but whatever it was, the end result was some fascinating vehicles . . . in spite of all the poverty.

You sat high in this old Auburn. You don't notice that when you look at the car, or even when you stand right up next to it—its lines are so good. In fact it was only when I drove out into traffic that I realized I was looking down on most of the present-day drivers—and that they were looking up at me . . . with some awe, I believe.

I nursed the car along, for quite a while thru traffic—remembering Wittenberg's plea to "please take it easy." I wanted to get used to the car before I let it out any. Besides, if you're like me, you would as soon trip your dainty old grandmother as treat a classic like the Auburn roughly.

I tried the brakes—at the first stop light —and they were really touchy. The car was only moving about 20 mph and the Auburn stopped with a jolt—but without nose-dive. In case you've forgotten, Auburn was among the first cars in this country to come out with full hydraulics. I tried braking a couple of times more at several different speeds so as to get the feel. Then I began to fool around with the center gear shift, moving the lever up and down between 2nd and 3rd as the Auburn wended its way thru back streets. (Once again Chesebrough and I were looking for photographic backgrounds.)

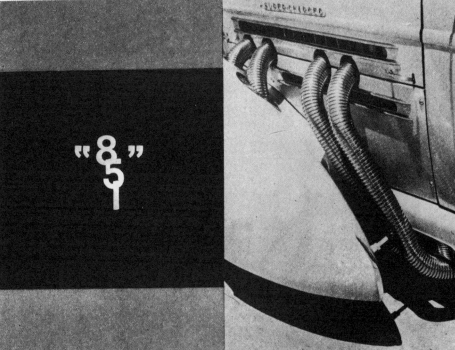

The 851 had a very interesting gear arrangement—a combination of a conventional (syncro-mesh) gearbox with dual-ratio rear-axle. This was to give you a town-speed and a highway speed. This business was controlled by a sliding clutch which was in turn activated by a vacuum cylinder fastened to the front of the axle housing. On the steering wheel horn-mount is a lever which, in one position, gives you at least 60 mph at 3000 rpm (according to the very beautiful tachometer on the dashboard) and perfectly amazing acceleration in town—and even up hills. The other ratio (brought into play by moving the lever) I didn't use much—Los Angeles traffic being what it is. But we know the engine peaks at 4000 rpm and there is a personally autographed silver plaque on the passenger's side of the cockpit which bears a legend signed with the he-man scrawl of Ab Jenkins—testifying that "This Auburn Automobile has been driven 100.9 mph before shipment from the Factory." So you slide rule fiends get to work and find the optium axle ratio, if you can.*

In our search for beautiful backgrounds, Chesebrough and I found our way out of the residential district and up into the oil-derrick be-studded Baldwin Hills which lie between Hollywood and Long Beach. And we got our eyes thoroly opened by the Auburn. The only other car of this make that I ever rode in was a sedan owned (at least fifth-hand) by a mechanic in my home town. This fellow had let the local sheriff use the car to chase after an escapee from the city jail—and the sheriff ran into a cow in the process. It didn't do the cow much harm, but by the time I rode in the Auburn its handling characteristics were somewhat altered for the worse.

When the curves came up in front of Bud Wittenberg's 851, Chesebrough and I really got tickled. We cranked thru the first bend (and a fairly sharp one at that) at about 35 mph . . . with the result that I oversteered all over the place. The Auburn roadster came right around—flat as a pancake. 35 mph doesn't sound like a very glamorous figure to you, I know, but try keeping that averag around the block in your family

CONTINUED ON PAGE 15

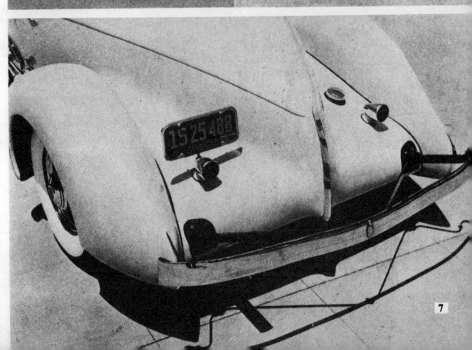

Salon

Tyrone Power's J-2 Duesenberg

Tyrone Power's

J-2 Duesenberg

Back in the days when we were kids—or at least a lot younger than we are now; when icy fingers of the Great Depression crept hungrily into nearly every family and home in the land; the great Duesenberg was rumbling its ponderous way along the roads and race circuits of the world*.

J. L. Elbert, in his superb book, "Duesenberg—America's Mightiest Motor Car" (Post Publ.), has told the story of the breed more thoroly than anyone ever has, or will. Rather than try to compete with Elbert's monumental research into the subject, I'll give you my impressions of one particular car—that owned by Hollywood's Tyrone Power.

I had never driven one of these great 6300 pound monstors. I grew up, as most of you did, hearing fabulous tales of Fred Duesenberg's amazing creation, but it was not until 20th Century Fox's Jimmie Talmadge invited me to try out Power's car that I finally got my hands on a Duesenberg steering wheel.

I met Jimmie at Tyrone Power's nifty pink bungalow (you should live in such a bungalow!) in the swank Bel Air—filmland's living room. When I told Jim what I wanted—some photography for the enthusiasts to drool over and some interesting facts for the readers—he pointed out, quite logically, that there was no better place in the world to shoot pictures than the Fox film lot. So, we all (Chesebrough, his camera, Talmadge, and I) climbed up into the Duesenberg and made off for the studio.

We got away so fast that I forgot all about the famous statue of Mrs. Power which is supposed to stand in the garden back of the movie star's house. According to the newspapers, Mrs. P. had her figure copied in the altogether and presented it to her spouse as a birthday present. I missed seeing the carving, but Power has a XX-120. Maybe Chesebrough and I can go back to Bel Air and do a story on the Jaguar next month.**

I wish I could tell you that the Duesenberg, for all its weight and 153 inch wheelbase, was as light handling as a sports car—but I can't. That would be stretching things too much. It was only a few blocks to the studios, but driving that distance was enough to get a clear picture of the J's maneuverability.

However, that was about the only fault I could find with the car . . . its size. If you remember . . . the thirties saw a world wide craze for great big cars. Every country had 'em. The Americans were no different than anybody else. We just went everybody one better.

But if the Duesenberg was ponderous to steer and drive, it is still one of the most

* Never mind the Great American Tragedy, Dearborn, just tell the readers about the car.—Ed. Billingsley.

** Oh, no you don't Dearborn! Next month you go to Watkins Glen—Billingsley.

Tyrone Power's J-2 Duesenberg

interesting cars I ever laid eyes on. On the Fox lot, while Chesebrough punched his shutter, Jimmie Talmadge went over the car with a fine toothed comb—briefing me on the details.

Old German-born Fred Duesenberg wasn't much of a hand to cut corners when he built a car. When he drew up a design; if he wanted a gadget on one of his creations, he simply installed one. Of course, he charged for it. $18,500 Power's car cost— new. So maybe the buyer was entitled to a little something . . . an extra novelty or two.

You probably remember that the quoted horsepower of the gigantic 8 cylinder, dual overhead cam engine was 265 at 4200 rpm. Fact is, the actual power curves show a rating of 207 hp at 3600 rpm . . . but that's plenty, even by today's standards. But what actually rocked me back on my heels was the mechanism which took care of the chassis lubrication. This little mechanical mind, mounted on the left side of the engine, gave a click every 85 miles and the chassis got a shot of oil. The driver didn't have to worry about a thing—except to lubricate the steering box. Carrying out the motif for relieving the owner of worry were the thermostatically operated louvers in front of the radiator, and the set of lights on the instrument panel which, at regular intervals, reminded you with a flash that the battery should be checked or the engine oil changed.

In spite of all this, the Duesenberg wasn't cheap to maintain. A valve job, for instance, was a very costly proposition—even at the lowest of depression prices. And there weren't a half a dozen men in the country who would (or could) take the time to do a decent job of it. To successfully complete a valve grind the mechanic had to maintain a chart as he went along—keeping track of the shims he removed to set the clearances correctly. It was an involved and tedious job, and one which had to be done correctly if "J" was to operate at peak performance.

Power's car lists officially as a Convertible Berline—which suited the snobbery of everybody in the mad Thirties—and it had an all aluminum body . . . except for the fenders. These massive members were steel, of course. Back of the rear seat was what Jimmie Talmadge called "the cocktail lounge". All you had to do was pull the back of the rear seat forward to expose a shelf of bottles and glasses. We pulled on the seat but there was nothing in the glasses.

In the driver's compartment was a feast for the enthusiast's eyes. The Duesenberg had a really complete set of instruments. Most cars — even twenty years ago — had speedometers, oil pressures fuel, water temperature gauges, and ammeters — but the Duesenberg started with these and went on with a 5000 rpm tachmeter, altimeter, brake pressure gauge . . . and *four* lights which periodically flashed on to remind you to service the car. If you had engine trouble, or got lost, Fred Duesenberg wanted to be sure it was your fault—not his.

I don't know about you, but I'm light happy. The more lights a car has the better I like it . . . particularly, good driving lights. On Power's car there is a mess of them. Two Lucas P-100's take care of the headlight department—tho they're not stock—and there are two marvelous driving lights with a bubble level mounted in their upper rims . . . all the easier to make daylight adjustments. Then on the cowl were mounted two Lorraine spots. In the rear, of course, the traditional Duesenberg combination back-up, stop-lights stuck out like a sore thumb.

Even tho it's old and maybe outdated in its size, Tyrone Power can be mighty proud of this old car . . . the remnant of a great and tragic age when the world was bravely blustering its way out of its blackest economic confusion.—R.D.

The background for Tyrone Power's J-2 Duesenberg is a Chinese set used in the new 20th Century-Fox picture "Sixty Saddles to Gobi".

Salon

The Classic Cord

To the purist, Bud Sennett's modified Cord may be an affront. He readily admits that the port holes were only incorporated after long deliberation and that most people think it should not have been done.

Bud, though a well known race car driver, is not wealthy, so he felt that his only car would have to be modified to suit his individual needs.

Originally the Cord was the comparatively rare convertible coupe, easily distinguishable from the convertible phaeton sedan by its provision for two persons only (plus a rumble seat). Bud added a jump seat and had the top bows re-worked to give headroom. The result may not be "pure", but it does give a neat club convertible.

The same practicality of reasoning influenced adaption of non-standard bumpers. Frankly, the original bumpers were "soft", and after recurring damage at both front and rear Bud installed a set of honest spring steel bars from a 1941 Olds.

During the war, and for most of the time since, Bud Sennett has been a flight-line mechanic for North American. As a result, the Cord is in near perfect mechanical condition. As an ex-race car driver and mechanic it was also inevitable that improvements would be made. A Cadillac carburetor is used and the distributor has had a modern vacuum-retard diaphram added. These changes give not only a slightly better performance but also improve gasoline economy—up to 17 miles per gallon at normal highway cruising speeds. A spare engine and complete transmission reposes in the garage, the latter in particular having a well known reputation for dental troubles. Some Cord owners have installed mechanical linkages to replace the electro-magnetic-vacuum system supplied as original gear shifting equipment. This is supposed to prolong gear tooth life by eliminating the "clunk", but Bud says that correct adjustment of the original mechanism will give a slight delay in shifting, regardless of how quickly the tiny electric hand is shifted. He has had transmission trouble only once—he

Comprehensive instrumentation layout of the Cord. Finger tip shift was designed to encourage use of 4-speeds by lazy U.S. drivers.

left the car parked in second gear and of course someone rammed the car hard enough to break off a tooth.

The 810 Cord was a completely new automobile from stem to stern. As is well known, Gordon M. Buehrig was responsible for the styling—his original design patent being filed on May 17, 1934 and issued on October 2 of that year. A revised design was filed and issued in 1935, both of these appearing in that very complete book "The Classic Cord".

The Lycoming Division of the Cord Corporation designed an entirely new V8 engine for this car. The bore and stroke was 3½ x 3¾, giving 286.6 cu. in. displacement, and it developed 125 bhp at 3500 rpm. An L-head valve arrangement was used but the valves were positioned horizontally and operated by rocker arms located just above the camshaft. This gives an odd shaped combustion chamber which in turn necessitated specially shaped piston crowns.

Along with the completely new V8 engine the '36 Cord design concept called for a considerable departure in the transmission department. To provide adequate leg room on a 125 inch wheelbase front wheel drive car, and to concentrate weight on the forward driving wheels the transmission was placed ahead of the differential. The drive goes from the engine (located behind the differential) forward to the transmission main shaft. Each one of the four forward speeds has its own main shaft gear and corresponding driven gear on the countershaft below. The drive goes from mainshaft to countershaft and thence aft to the differential pinion gear.

The 810 Cord chassis carried a unique single trailing arm independent front suspension using a transverse leaf spring mounted below the arms. Wheel bump travel was transmitted to the spring via short "tension rods" with rubber insulators at each end.

The performance of the Cord V8 models has been the subject of too much speculation. Company literature carried some amazing contradictions. At one point they say of the top speed—"about 100 mph" (unsupercharged). Yet their own published power required vs power available curves show a definite intersection at 93 mph. This latter figure is corroborated by the British

The "plumbing" of the 125 horsepower Cord engine makes one wonder how they ever found room for the supercharger installation.

"Autocar" road test of May 29, 1936 when the average of four timed runs gave 89.78 mph, with the best run at 92.18 mph. The speedometer incidently read just 10 mph fast during these runs.

Great controversy rages over the top speed of the 1937 supercharged model. A British road test of that year gave 102.27 mph as the best of 4 runs which averaged 98.90 mph. The official American stock car record stands at 107.66 mph, held by a factory tuned car, certified as stock by the AAA. Ab Jenkins the driver says the car would do slightly over 120 mph, but that tire treads just wouldn't stay on.

The writer has contacted numerous ex-factory personnel in an atempt to trace the story of "200 bhp—120 mph" model Cords. Three of these people were at one time or another in the position of Chief Engineer at Lycoming and all three agree that to the best of their knowledge the above figures are exaggerated. Nevertheless the performance of the *170 bhp* Cord is still an experience, zero to 60 mph in 13.2 seconds for example, is a time equalled by only two or three of our top entrants in the horsepower race.

Perhaps the Cord can best be summaribed by quoting from Dan Post's book, "The Classic Cord." Seeing the car for the first time, someone said, "It didn't look like an automobile. Somehow it looked like a beautiful thing that had been born and just grew up on the highway." J.B.

1936 Cord Specifications

wheelbase	125 in.
tread, front	56 in.
rear	61 in.
tire size	6.50 - 16
weight, standard	3934 lbs.
supercharged	4016 lbs.
approx distribution	55/45
bore	3.50 in.
stroke	3.75 in.
cu. in.	288.6
comp. ratio	6.5
no. main bearings	3
bearing dia.	2.50 in.
engine wt.	566 lbs.
clutch	Long—10 in.
trans. make	Detroit Gear
gear ratios (O.A. with 43/10 gears)	
1st	9.077
2nd	5.848
3rd	3.884
4th	2.748
U-Joint make	Rzeppa
brake drums	11 x 2¼
front spring	34¼ x 2½
rear springs	54½ x 2
hp req'd at 60 mph (from catalog)	22.5
hp req'd at 60 mph (from Co. curves)	40.0

13

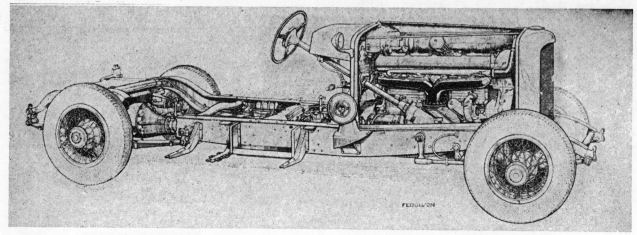

A rare chassis drawing showing one of the few RHD Duesenbergs exported to England. (From the Autocar for May 2, 1930).

MISC. RAMBLINGS

. . . By the Tech. Ed.

In this column last March we instituted something new—a *Road and Track* Performance Factor. The utility of any performance factor is to enable assessment and comparison of car performance on paper—working only with the specifications.

The British use a factor known as litres per ton mile, while American engineers prefer cubic feet of explosion volume per ton mile. Both of these factors assume that the peak torque per cubic inch (or bmep if you wish) is the same for all engines. Now that almost every company publishes the peak torque and rpm figure for its engines, it is possible to use the torque data for more accurate comparisons. The result is a number —an index of performance. By arbitrarily setting up the Cadillac Allard as 100, we arrive at a constant of 300 in the formula, and any other car can be compared as above or below a norm of 100. To repeat the formula we have:

$$PF = \frac{\text{Torque x axle ratio x wheel revs/mile}}{300 \text{ x (curb weight} + 300 \text{ lbs.)}}$$

For a Cadillac-Allard the problem is as follows:

$$PF = \frac{312 \text{ x } 3.54 \text{ x } 738}{300 (2408 + 300)} = 100$$

It is feasible to compare P.F. in any gear, but the rating obtained is good for that gear only. In other words, two cars with identical high gear performance factors would have nearly identical high gear acceleration. Yet, one might have vastly superior acceleration through the gears, where better indirect ratios and horsepower to weight ratio are of importance.

The Duesenberg model J and JS cars are held in high esteem by many people, including the writer. Nevertheless, like all cars (so it seems), they had their shortcomings and idiosyncrasies. Among the many myths concerning this car was the actual developed bhp of 265 claimed for the J. In 1939 I obtained through a close friend, an actual power curve of a 1929 production engine— engine number J-110 to be exact. Digging through the old files at Lycoming (who, as a division of the Cord Corporation, built all the J engines), this friend obtained the data reproduced herewith—the best of 4 engines which were checked during that year.

Disillusioned? So was I. Notice that the

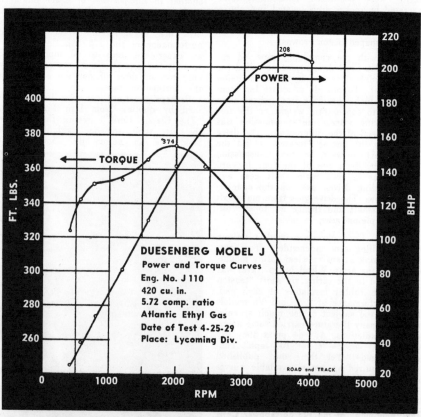

DUESENBERG MODEL J
Power and Torque Curves
Eng. No. J 110
420 cu. in.
5.72 comp. ratio
Atlantic Ethyl Gas
Date of Test 4-25-29
Place: Lycoming Div.

Disappointment over the peak power of the unblown Duesenberg is partially alleviated by the high torque curve. The supercharged SJ is said to have developed about 265 bhp.

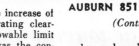

peak power was 208 bhp at 3600 rpm, and the peak torque is a very healthy 374 ft/lbs. at 2000 rpm. There is a very obvious reason for this discrepancy, for I feel that Fred Duesenberg realized that torque was more important that horsepower to the average man. While his engine was certainly capable of delivering 265 bhp at 4200 rpm (with proper valve timing), he deliberately used a very conservative valve timing (5°-45°-45°-5°) to boost the low speed torque. I think we can safely say that prior to the recent trend toward automatic transmissions, nearly all automobile manufacturers have been at one time or another guilty of advertising a boost in bhp, when actually they had only increased their engine's torque. Today's shiftless drives make low speed torque of less importance than it used to be, a fact which is readily borne out by noting the "full race" valve timings of our new ohv V-8 engines.

When the Society of Automotive Engineers holds a meeting, the carefully prepared papers presented may or may not be too interesting, but the discussions which follow are often extremely lively. Currently there is much spirited sparring going on among the engineers over mechanical vs. chemical octanes (Chrysler vs. GM). The somewhat hushed subject of lead deposits from Ethyl gasoline is also getting a much needed airing.

An example of opposed thinking comes to light by comparing the remarks of Chrysler's Zeder on cost savings possibilities of smaller cars (*Road and Track*, March, 1953) to that of W. D. Appel of Ford. Mr. Appel says, "The only way to reduce operating costs is to make light cars with lower performance standards. This inevitably leads to a smaller car. And you reduce the price of the car by having fewer and simpler parts. *Here again size reduction of parts helps.*"

The remarks of Harry Toulmin of the Ethyl Corporation on the Jaguar XK-120 are extremely interesting. "The Jag. is about 300 pounds lighter than a standard Chevrolet and has an engine of 6 cu in. less displacement (1952 model—Ed.)."

"The car is extremely stable, can negotiate highway turns at 80 to 100 mph with practically no roll or sway. It's possible to accelerate smoothly in top gear from 10 mph to the car's top speed of 120 mph."

"The car has excellent brakes. so that high road speeds are possible with safety. *but by U. S. standards, the engine and gearbox are quite noisy and the ride harsh.*"

Few will quarrel with the above (as far as it goes), but a Packard executive's statement in a recent press interview relative to foreign cars is pure hogwash. "The car (re ferring to a Bentley) just couldn't compare with our Packard Clipper."

While imported cars have brought a tremendous surge of public interest in cars that are different; the sales totals are still a mere trickle. This fact should not detract from Henry Ford II's recent statement urging extension of free trade throughout the free world. Very commendable.

Having a column labelled "Misc. Ramblings" is wonderful for a harassed (by letters—I got thousands of them) Tech. Ed. From foreign trade policy I can go straight to aluminum alloy connecting rods.

Franklin probably pioneered the light alloy connecting rod, and promptly ran into trouble. With the normal .002 diametral clearance at room temperature, the lower end expanded with oil temperature rise. From 70° F to a readily attained tempera-

ture of 200° F gives a clearance increase of .0016. This meant a total operating clearance of .0036—close to the allowable limit for noise. Even more serious was the contraction at below zero ambient temperatures. The engine could not be cranked.

The Bohn Aluminum Company solved this problem very neatly by making the rod cap a steel forging. This forced the aluminum half of the bearing to conform to the more rigid cap. Among the users of "dural" rods were Hupmobile, Lycoming (Auburn, Elcar, Gardner, etc.), Stutz, Duesenburg, and Nash. Other problems remained; namely, the difficulty of getting a reliable bond between the babbitt and the aluminum, and more serious—fatigue failure. Recent developments in high strength aluminum alloys, improved techniques in eliminating stress concentrations and replaceable bearing inserts makes the use of dural rods practical. The only trouble is—why bother. The modern large bore short stroke engine has such a large portion of the reciprocating mass in the piston that weight saving in the rod is not worthwhile. The new Buick rod, for instance, is only 6 inches long.

Where cost is no object, there is one facet of the dural rod that is most interesting. This is the possibility of eliminating all special bearing alloys and running the rod directly on the crankpin. Aluminum with 7% of tin added makes a very good heavy duty bearing. Rolls Royce in England and Alcoa in America did considerable research work with this alloy—even before the war. The 1938 Lagonda V-12 used dural rods, running directly on the crankpins, as did the Leland diesel. The Triumph motorcycle has, since 1937, used a plain dural rod with a babbitt-lined steel cap. Many small air-cooled industrial engines (Wisconsin and others) use this construction very successfully. The only precaution required is a little more running clearance than usual, plus a crankpin surface at least as hard as obtained with a cast steel crankshaft (about 300 Brinell). Makes an interesting possibility for high speed engines—no bearing to burn out. •

sedan and you'll see what I mean.

I looked at Chesebrough and he grinned back at me. So we tried the next corner a little faster. The Auburn straightened that one out just as neatly. By this time I had the feel of the car and felt right at home. We found out that you could point the long hood at a corner in real sports car fashion and the 851 would come right around in absolute safety. Above a certain speed the rear end had a tendency to skip if the road was a little rough, as did most pre-war sports cars. But you'll recognize that as characteristic—and forgivable in a car of this vintage.

Bud had sworn there was plenty of gas in the tank, but after cruising rather aimlessly for a couple of hours we pulled into a service station—just to be on the safe side. Chesebrough climbed out and headed toward the Coke machine while I sat and waited for the attendant to come over and admire the car . . . I figured he would.

But he was one of those lads all of us can do without. He stared out the window of the station for a minute, trying to decide whether or not we wanted anything worth his while. Then he ambled over toward me —giving first me and then the car one of "those" looks. He was in full possession of himself as he moved close to the car and stopped . . . waiting for me to say what I wanted. I suppose I didn't speak up quickly enough, because he sighed disdainfully and very patiently pulled a grimy paw out of his pocket. Then, so help me, he leaned his hand very squarely on one of the Auburn's hot, gleaming, chrome exhaust pipes—where they protrude from the hood. May I say that that changed his mood? He was most respectful to the Auburn as he filled the tank and checked the tires. When we drove away he was eyeing his customized coupe . . . somewhat shaken too, he was.

Before the sun had sunk too low for proper exposures, Chesebrough had found a location to his liking. We "shot" the Auburn and headed back for Cavalier Motors (Bud's foreign car showroom). On the way we had a chance to let the Auburn out a bit and it is no exaggeration to say that the faster it moved, the smoother it became—with steering at all speeds as light as a feather.

It sort of makes you wonder what kind of car Auburn would be building today if they had stayed in business. If they had taken that same car and improved it in accordance with twenty years' experience, it seems to me America might well be mass producing a *genuine* sports car today—a car that would be a real pleasure to own and drive.

—ROBERT DEARBORN

others are classic touring specials . . .

Not a Bugatti Royale, but a 142 inch Duesenberg with a custom built roadster body.

DUESENBERG J

by Hudson Mills

Photographs by Henry Weller

Redesigned Duesenberg is 42" high at the radiator cap, has steel fenders, aluminum body.

Road and Track readers will remember the owner of this car from his article on Bugatti models which appeared in our November 1953 issue. Even a casual Bugatti addict cannot help but notice the "family resemblance" of this special bodied J Duesenberg to some of the immortal products of Molsheim. This is not a coincidence, though the actual process of designing such a similar body was probably not intentional. I recall the first time I met Hudson, very well. It was at Watkins Glen, back in the days when this was the premiere sports car road race—as well as a mecca of mechanical oddities. Hudson was peering under some unlucky fellow's pride and joy, a Bugatti of course, muttering all the while to himself. Maybe some clot had put a type 44 front axle under a 35 B chassis, I don't recall, but I do know that Hudson Mills is a perfectionist. Whether it is one of his Bugattis, his 2.3 Alfa Romeo, or this Model J, the job is done right. J.B.

When I first saw my Duesenberg chassis in December, 1945, it was quite sad—it had been standing in dead storage for seven years. I won't go into detail to try to tell you how really bad it looked, but it seemed to brighten up just a little when I tried to fill the tires. Even though they had been flat for many years they filled readily and what still seems odd to me, held the pressure for months after.

Not wanting to ready it for the road or take a chance on firing up as it was, we towed it to a friend's garage where the heavy and one time expensive town sedan body was removed; then it was towed to my garage for a major rebuild of the engine and chassis.

The engine and transmission were removed and completely disassembled under the guid-

16

This shows the staggering size and semi-modern lines of Hudson Mill's J Duesenberg.

ance of a late associate and friend of the Duesenberg brothers, namely, Shirley Mitchell, who in my estimation was the greatest living authority on Duesenbergs until his death two years ago. Shirley could tell you the number and size of threads and just what kind of a trick wrench to use on every nut and bolt in that motor. He had facts, figures and clearances at his finger tips, and most important, the history behind them of every bearing and working part in an S or SJ. Both the engine and myself profited greatly from his knowledge.

To continue, we disassembled the engine and transmission, washed and scrutinized every part. Anything that was worn we replaced. New domed pistons, pins, rings, etc. were fitted with the proper clearances be-

tween the small ends and piston bosses. All new main and connecting rod bearings were hand fitted and lapped in to secure 100% bearing surface. The fitting of all bearings, pistons, etc. as well as the complete assembly was done by Jack Donaldson and his son John under Mitchell's eye. After the pistons, rods, bearings etc. were assembled and before assembly on the crankshaft each of the eight units were weighed on an apothecary's scale and each assembled unit adjusted to weigh the same.

Then came the job of installing it back in the chassis. Have you ever tried moving a buttoned-up Duesey engine? It's really a load. The chassis meantime had been cleaned and sanded after shortening 10" to 142". All the old one-shot oil lines and retainers

were removed and new Alemite fittings installed. The hypoid rear end was cleaned and inspected and found ok. Hydraulic brake parts were renewed, new Bendix booster, etc. The wheels were cut down to 16" using widebase drop-center rims and 7.00 tires. The clutch appeared to be new and transmission was happily in very good condition.

We used the old Schebler updraft carburetor (which according to many is far better suited to this engine than the later model downdraft Stromberg) and the engine fired up instantly. It made an awful racket, but had a beautiful rythm. Took me back quite a few years when I used to hear the Dueseys being tested in the old plant in Elizabeth, N. J., long before the brothers moved west.

The engine has gone only 600 miles to date at not over 2500 rpm and now has a new four port balanced aluminum manifold using four special racing sidedraft Solex carburetors, installed.

The original radiator, after cleaning and checking, was lowered so the top is only three feet six inches from the ground. Of course this height was accomplished only after the body was built and springs flattened. New header pipes, twin tail pipes and a special straight through stainless steel packed muffler were fabricated.

The body was drawn to scale, but changes and refinements during construction were drawn on the cement floor. The body frame is made of chrome molybdenum tubing covered with 16 gauge half-hard aluminum. Fenders are steel. Instruments are new standard Duesenberg with needle tachometer and speedometer, all set in Honduras mahogany dashboard. The upholstery is top grain cowhide in natural color. The rear deck is finished in quilted Boliflex and the floor carpeting is triple twist broadloom.

Until we get this automobile to a dynamometer the horse power will have to be estimated. Anyway it is plenty high as can be experienced from the driver's seat, even though still not fully run-in. ●

A concourse winning interior which features a solid mahogany instrument panel, Brooklands type steering wheel, and original instruments.

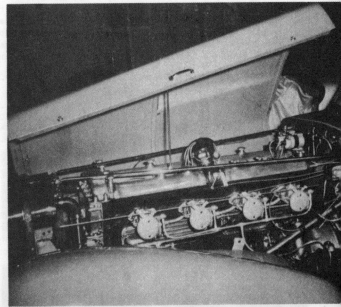

The immense 420 cu in. (6885 cc) engine literally dwarfs the four special Solex carburetors. Estimated bhp is well over 265.

Salon

AUBURN V-12 SPEEDSTER

Beautiful car, dubious classic

Many times a review of past events and happenings produces strange conclusions which are not easy to understand, in the cold light of hindsight rather than foresight.

The Auburn V-12 is one of these—it happened, but it shouldn't have. Along with all other car producers of 1930 and 1931, the Auburn Company felt, to some extent, the economic pressure of the period. Like many others, they saw fit to introduce larg-er, more luxurious, more expensive cars at a time when the market for such had virtually disappeared. Perhaps their management felt that their sales gains made in 1931 (while others were going down) justified the move.

Whatever their reasons, the Auburn V-12 of 1932 was a fabulous machine for the time. Its 160 bhp was exceeded by only a handful of cars, all selling for two to five times the price asked for the Auburn.

(List price of the Speedster was $1845!) The 1933 Speedster model, as shown here, was just capable of exceeding an honest 100 mph in full touring trim, for in July of 1932 a strictly stock model achieved 100.74 mph for the flying kilometer and averaged 92.2 for one hour running at Bonneville under AAA sanction. In December a "stripped" model, running without fenders, windshield etc., reached 118.32 mph and averaged 109.33 mph for 12 hours.

The Lycoming V-12 engine was a lot of machinery for the money.

A non-standard instrument panel is an affront to the purist.

Iron bars do not a prison make—nor do boat-tails make a sports car, necessarily.

The Lycoming designed and built V-12 engine was called every name imaginable —from "a hunk of useless cast iron" to "an engineering masterpiece." Owners' reports, at the time, were not overwhelmingly enthusiastic but most of the complaints came from those who were unwilling to pay the extra charge for the optional 2-speed rear axle and were getting 10 mpg or less, as a result. The engine was huge, 391 cu in. to be exact (3.125" x 4.25"), and had a massive crankshaft with 4 main bearings, 3" in diameter. Combustion chambers were unique, the result of using horizontal valves actuated by a single camshaft and rocker arms located within the Vee formed by the cylinder banks. Although the cylinder heads were detachable, a unique feature was six individual water jacketed castings bolted to the heads at each pair of cylinders in such a way that valves could be serviced without removing the main head castings. Each sub-head casting also carried two spark plug bosses. When demand dwindled for the passenger car (only 404 cars were built in 1933) this powerplant was later offered as a marine conversion and a few were used to power fire-engines.

In spite of its 160 bhp (at 3500 rpm) the standard axle ratio was 4.55 to 1 and a stock sedan would barely exceed an honest 90 mph, the engine turning an astronomical (for the time) 4500 rpm. The two speed axle completely transformed the car and gave a choice of 4.55 to 1 or 3.04 to 1 ratio. Performance was excellent, even in the high ratio and claims of up to 15/16 mpg were made by owners—under favorable conditions.

The Auburn V-12 is unquestionably a questionable classic. While it was an interesting car, with many qualities considered essential for classic car status, it fell far short on quality. There are even those who maintain that this car was a piece of junk! We take no sides here. —J.B. ●

Salon

DUESENBERG

The aristocratic Rollston "J"

photography: Ralph Poole

OF ALL THE cars built during the "golden era" of motoring, the classic Duesenberg model J stands out in size, appearance, engineering and performance. The Bugatti Royale exceeded the J in size, the Hispano-Suiza V-12 would accelerate more rapidly (but was not as fast), the 2.9 Alfa-Romeo had at least an equal engineering interest, and several American cars of the period were perhaps equally good looking. But the Duesenberg, like her contemporary, Jean Harlow, literally and figuratively "had everything".

Strangely enough America's greatest classic was also one of the least understood by laymen. In fact, according to J. E. Elbert in his priceless book, "Duesenberg, the Mightiest American Motor Car", there is at least one Duesenberg owner who insists his car was built in Germany, and examples of similar misinformation have often appeared in fictional writings.

The original announcement of the model J appeared in December of 1928, with the heading, "265 bhp, 116 mph". In June of 1932 a supercharged version was introduced (the "SJ") with 320 bhp. It was stated to be capable of accelerating from a stand-still to 100 mph in 17 seconds and on the basis of its power to weight ratio (about 17 lbs/hp) it should. No one has ever obtained a timed top speed on either the J or the SJ but a little slide-rule work indicates the claimed 130 mph for the more-powerful model is definitely optimistic for a fully equipped sedan or coupe—but still only by about 10 mph.

Competition activities of the Big J appear to have been limited to Le Mans where Prince Nicolas of Rumania ran two years in succession, but did not finish either time. There was a match race once, between Phil Berg's J and Harpo Marx's big 6 Mercedes SS. It was a 25 mile event on

the flats of Muroc dry lake and the Duesenberg won by default when the Merk lost its blower. Average speed quoted at the time was 104 mph.

Fred Duesenberg, the car's designer was a superb engineer with an instinct for "rule-of-thumb" design which concealed his genuine knowledge. He was ably assisted by his chief designer William R. Beckman and his brother August Duesenberg who died only recently. Beckman translated the ideas onto paper and "Augie's" flair for making things work, completed the near-perfect team—ideas, design and development.

Design work on the "J" began in the spring of 1927 and four experimental engines were built. Data on two of these engines was published in the S.A.E. Journal for December 1928, with emphasis on the advantages of the four-valve (per cylinder) head as compared to the two-valve head. The latter developed 143 bhp at 3500, while

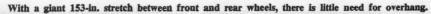

With a giant 153-in. stretch between front and rear wheels, there is little need for overhang.

In spite of car's enormous size, the narrow radiator and graceful fenders never suggest bulk.

the 4-valve engine developed 194 bhp at 4100 rpm and had a peak torque of 336 ft-lbs at 1600 rpm. The production engines had a larger cylinder bore, and while the peak horsepower may have been a little short of claims, the conservative valve timing chosen gave the truly astounding torque figure of 374 ft-lbs at 2000 rpm. (See R & T for May, 1953, page 33).

In some ways the "J" was not unlike its contemporary, the 8-litre Bentley, for both cars offered a very much higher performance than the Rolls-Royce, but in so doing they also lost a certain amount of refinement in smooth running qualities. The 6.9 litre "J" engine was powerful and efficient, but under full-throttle it was also somewhat noisy and rough-running. Lengthy conversations with the road test personnel at A.C.D. in Auburn (during 1935/36) also elicited the information that the massive J-chassis still left something to be desired and considerable testing was being done to reduce what these hypercritical men called "front-end flap" at speeds of around 100 mph. Nevertheless, for a chassis of the early thirties the Duesenberg was an advanced design, and in retrospect any deficiencies can be blamed on the attendent problems of size and speed well beyond the norm. Without a doubt the Duesenberg could cruise at 80 or even 90 mph in greater safety and comfort and with less effort or strain than any other American candidate for the title "the Supreme Classic".

Fuel consumption was of course another matter, even though unimportant to the man who could afford one. The normal range appears to have been between 7 and 10 miles per gallon, though the catalog does say "the car is surprisingly economical of fuel, averaging 11 to 13 miles per gallon at 50 miles per hour".

When first announced, the chassis price was given as $8500, but this was raised to $9500 in 1929. The "chassis" included four fenders, 6 chrome-plated wire wheels and a fully equipped instrument panel supported by an enormous aluminum casting which formed the toe and dash-boards and carried all the wiring in covered passages. Bodies

Seen from the right, the huge 6.9 litre engine displays polished aluminum dohc covers, dual headers and tapered water manifold.

On the left side can be seen more aluminum and the Stromberg dual-downdraft carburetor, which was installed only on the last cars built.

Even more chrome than Detroit's best, but it never has that "stuck-on" look.

Front suspension incorporates Watson Stabilators.

were of course extra, but certain types were more or less standardized. Prices with body varied from $14,750 to $17,750 f.o.b. Indianapolis, but an occasional "one-off" body sold for a little more.

Without a doubt it would cost two and more likely three times as much today to duplicate the Duesenberg car in the same quantities (about 470 cars were built). Since our present system of taxation makes it impossible for all but a handful of executives to earn the requisite $30,000 (net) in any one year, it is unlikely that we will ever again see such a car as this, produced for sale.

The beautifully restored example shown here carries engine No. J-337 in a long chassis (153.5 in w.b.) with convertible victoria body by Rollston. As most of the Rollston convertibles had the "blind" type top this "quarter-window" type is especially rare. In a day when restoration to "concours condition" is fast becoming commonplace, this car commands respect; at the 1955 Pebble Beach event it ran a close second to the overall show winner (Phil Hill's Pierce-Arrow). Its proud owner is James G. Aiken, who owns an Oldsmobile agency in Westwood, California. Mr. Aiken does not care to mention the cost of restoration, but two men working spare-time for 5 months will give an inkling of the outlay involved. ●

Flawless restoration includes interior; note aluminum dash with stop-watch clock, altimeter, brake pressure gauge.

Amid lush surroundings rises an emergency brake that no one need grope for.

photographs: courtesy R. W. Dwight

Auburn

WHEN THE 1928 Auburn cars were announced the advertising headlines said simply: announcing the 115 HORSE-POWER AUBURN in big bold type. This may not sound very startling today, but in those days even the big Auburn straight-8 was a moderately priced car and 100 horsepower was unknown, even in such expensive cars as Lincoln and Cadillac.

But Auburn had two more surprises in store, the first being the sensational 8-115 open speedster with its rakish V-windshield and boat tail body contours. But the climax was the 1929 Cabin Speedster shown here.

Wade Morton, a well known driver, was employed by Auburn at the time and many a Speedster owner will testify that the plaque on his car gave a certified speed of over 100 mph over the signature of Wade Morton. (Ab Jenkins also did this "work" at about the same time.) It was Wade Morton who conceived the idea of developing the open model still further and the Cabin Speedster was the result.

Auburn's literature on this striking car contains some interesting paragraphs, to wit:

"Here is tomorrow's automobile design. Not a fantastic dream of a groping modernist or futurist, but a practical reality based on scientific wind resistance.

"It is aptly named the Cabin Speedster, because—

"Present automobile styles are adaptations of the horse-and-buggy period; they have been dug out of the graves of an antiquated past; they are carry overs from the slow-age.

"Automobiles, as well as planes, must minimize wind resistance to attain increased speed. Automobiles, as well as planes, must also avoid the vacuum, or retarding suction of afterdrafts. With these aims we applied all that has been learned in years of automobile racing where reduced weight, the stream-lines and the pointed tails have made greater speed possible on speedways, and combined with those lessons, what aeronautical science has taught. The Cabin Speedster therefore is a subtle compound of racing car and aeroplane, sky-styled, designed by the famous racing driver and aviator, Wade Morton."

The wheelbase of the cabin speedster was reduced to 120 inches and the frame rails swept under the rear axle rather than over as on the open speedster. This facilitated the use of an underpan which extended the full length of the chassis. Cycle fenders mounted on the brake backing plates weighed only 9 pounds each and of course "moved" with the wheels. The body panels were aluminum but the tail piece consisted of a heavy bronze casting in lieu of bumpers. The body at its widest point was only 2" wider than the frame and frontal area was very low. The top of the radiator stood 44 inches above the ground while the overall height of the cab was only 58 inches. There were two seats only, described as "wicker basket aeroplane-type." The complete car with gas, oil and water weighed 3000 pounds.

The engine of the 8-125 was built by Lycoming and had cylinder dimensions of $3\frac{1}{4}$ x $4\frac{1}{2}$ inches. This was the same 298 cu. in. powerplant used at one time or another by Gardner, Elcar and others in-

cluding the front-wheel drive Cord. It was generally considered a good engine, in its hey-day and much better than the $2\frac{7}{8}$ x $4\frac{3}{4}$ inch powerplant of the cheaper 8-88 Auburn models.

Apparently only one Cabin Speedster was built and so far no one seems to know what happened to it. ●

Doorway of Auburn Automobile Co. plant at Auburn, Ind., taken over in 1938 by Dallas Winslow and now hqtrs. of A-C-D Co.

MAN OF MANY PARTS / *The Story of A-C-D*

Six-man staff includes (l. to r.) Silberg (body), Shoudek (engine), Butler (upholsterer), Carper (engine), McQuown (mechanic), Batdorf (transmission).

by Paul R. Hayes

THE MAN from Texas walked slowly all around the long, low car, and the black lacquer of the six-foot-long hood reflected his smile of satisfaction as he leaned over to pat the bulge that was the trademark of a front-drive. Still smiling, he entered the office and calmly counted out $3600—$500 more than his rebuilt Cord had cost new in 1929.

That scene, with an antique or classic car as the centerpiece, has been repeated on an average of fifteen times yearly since 1938 in a one-of-a-kind factory at Auburn, Indiana, where the necessary slow motion of fine craftsmanship balances the rarity of customers' moneybelts stuffed with $3,000 for one-shot transfusions.

No restrictions, however, curb activity in another section of the plant where ceiling-high bins are crammed with a million dollars in bits and pieces of some of the 1,900 automobiles whose names are all but forgotten. Thousands of parts, ranging from a five-cent gasket for a 1928 Stearns-Knight to a $250 transmission for the 1948 Tucker that never got into production, are shipped here annually to owners of fine, fancy and unusual cars who know the Auburn-Cord-Duesenberg Company as the only blood bank for their treasures.

The mastermind of all this is a man who began work as a piano key fitter in the early 1900s, rapidly became attuned to the business world and looks upon classic cars with the unesthetic detachment of one who considers the latest model Cadillac the ultimate in transportation.

He is Dallas Winslow, of Grand Blanc and Detroit, Michigan, who was born on Christmas day in 1893 and often plays Santa Claus to his 450 employees—whom he calls "associates"—in seven plants in Ohio, Michigan and Indiana. Being a merchant of bearings, pistons, nuts and

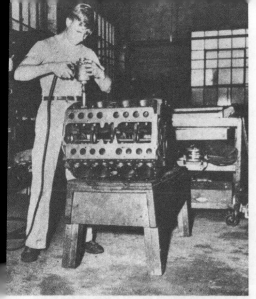

John McQuown uses a portable grinder to face the valve seats on Cord V-8 engine block.

Dwight Batdorf, shop foreman and transmission expert, goes to work on a Cord gearbox.

Ralph Butler, first with Auburn in 1909, applies his upholsterer's needle to a front seat.

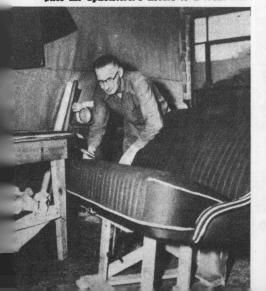

bolts and other hardware made for automotive machinery orphaned by bankruptcy is a sideline; his primary concern is the Mast-Foos Manufacturing Company, producer of lawnmowers and other power-driven garden equipment. A man whose passion for anonymity has made him probably the least-known philanthropist in the country, Winslow's share-the-wealth policies since 1921 have brought his "associates" hearing aids, dentures, eyeglasses, custom-made shirts, vacations in Florida, new automobiles and even ponies for their children.

The plight of the orphan car owner as a business possibility first caught Winslow's eye in 1929, six years after the 15-year-old Paterson breathed its last at Flint, Michigan. He bought the parts bins and set about soliciting business by a direct mailing to owners whose names were obtained by the simple, but time consuming, process of surveying state registration records.

That pattern was repeated as tombstones were erected in Flint, Cleveland, Lansing, Syracuse, Auburn, Indianapolis, Connersville, Detroit and Chicago over the corporate bodies of the Star, Stearns-Knight, Durant, air-cooled Franklin, Auburn, Duesenberg, Cord, Hupmobile, Graham and, more recently, even the much-ballyhooed, rear-engined Tucker of the last decade.

But it wasn't until 1938—when the automotive portion of the empire built by Errett Lobban Cord, one-time used car salesman whose golden touch also spanned airlines and a motor company by the time he was 39, was pushed into oblivion by the recession—that the operation began to breathe with gusto in the Mast-Foos money structure. In addition to the parts bins of the Auburn, Cord and Duesenberg, Winslow acquired the 36-year-old Auburn Automobile Company administration building, former headquarters of a firm that had proudly advertised certain of its models had been driven 100 miles an hour by the redoubtable Ab Jenkins.

To Winslow's amazement, the boat-tailed Auburn Speedster, front-drive Cord and 265-320 horsepower Duesenberg emerged as three items of automotive royalty, that strange breed which due to engineering, styling, handling or a combination of the three, set them apart as classic cars.

Literature, mailed under the newly-taken imprint of A-C-D, brought such a flood of response that the original plan to use the Auburn building's 70,000 square feet of floor space for lawnmower repair and parts storage was revised to include a clinic for ancient and cherished automobiles. Demand for service has been so great that four veteran Auburn employees, transferred to Winslow's payroll when he picked up the real estate, have been kept busy in "renewing department" for 16 years.

By 1946, the less abundant Duesenberg parts were depleted and re-sold to Marshall Merkes, Illinois industrialist and fancier of the marque who operates now from California as the Imperial Mfg. Co. The Auburn and Cord, riding on the crest of the classic car tide, represent the bulk of A-C-D business today although the Franklin's increasing popularity indicates it is fast becoming a hot collector's item. Altogether, half of the Auburn plant's still-increasing dollar volume is realized from the automotive parts and service section.

Restorations are undertaken on a basis of appointments scheduled as long as six months in advance with three of the popular but hard-to-come-by 1935-36 Speedsters booked annually. A dozen Cords also are rebuilt in an average year, the majority being the 1936 Model 810 and supercharged 812 models of 1937 although a surprising number of the 1929-32 L-29s also report for attention.

These patients wear license plates from all over the country and a few years ago one even arrived from Hawaii. Many wobble down Auburn's tree-lined streets with fenders flapping and engines rasping; the more decrepit arrive by truck, on the wrecker's hook and in railroad cars. But the chronic-

The 125 bhp V8 has been lifted from a Cord 810 preparatory to a complete overhaul. The convertible coupe in the background has been brought in for a periodic check-up.

ally disabled are only a trickle compared to the healthy models returned for a periodic checkup by proud owners who place all their faith with A-C-D specialists.

Bills of $3,000 are commonplace in the renewing department but the distinction as the heaviest spender rests with Cal Grosscup, Auburn tavern owner, who sold his late model Cadillac in 1952 and bought a Speedster and Model 810 Cord. When the factory had finished, he had $6,500 in the pair. Grosscup and his wife consider their money invested rather than spent since Auburn and Cord values increase rather than depreciate.

Not all wives share Mrs. Grosscup's enthusiasm, and there is at least one who thinks her spouse was only half as extravagant with his mechanical mistress as was actually the case. The factory, in the interest of keeping peace in the family of a good customer, aided in the deception by giving him two receipts, each for half of the total.

Despite the big money activity in restorations, the business in the shipping room rings the merriest tune on the cash registers. For every classic or antique car owner who can afford a factory rebuilding job, hundreds of less well-heeled do their own work in backyard garages and buy parts by mail as the family budget permits. For both, A-C-D is an oasis, and Winslow is the man who struck gold in the barren land of another's bankruptcy.

Those due for the full treatment are stripped with major components being distributed to four men whose total experience of 144 years makes them the nation's Auburn-Cord-Duesenberg experts. Ora Shoudel, who brought his tool kit to Auburn in 1926, takes over the engine; the transmission is the responsibility of Dwight Batdorf, shop foreman and veteran of 28 years; Russell Silberg, with Auburn 41 years, handles the body work and Ralph Butler, an artist with an upholsterer's needle, applies his 46 years' experience to the interior. These four are

Perfect specimens: Auburn and Cord restored by A-C-D and bought by Cal Grosscup for $6500.

assisted by Howard Carper and John McQuown, more recent additions to the staff.

Considering this kind of talent and the mechanical prima donnas on which they operate, a labor charge of $4 an hour is reasonable enough. The total of parts and service can add up fast however, and all terms are cash. Upholstering, using original patterns, cost $350. Rebuilt engine assemblies for the 125-horsepower V8 Cord run $310 and $40 more for the 175-horsepower supercharged version, both skeleton blocks without heads and accessories. The gigantic and more plentiful 115-150 horsepower straight-8 Auburn sells for $200 while the temperamental Cord transmission represents an investment of $254.

Since A-C-D relies heavily on the exchange system, E. C. Bartels, with Auburn since 1929 and director of sales, is confident the 1,800 Cords and 8,000 Auburns (most are of the less desirable models than the Speedster) still in existence will be drawing on the firm for replacement units ten years from now.

Bartels also estimates 30,000 Grahams and 23,000 Hupmobiles are on the highways and expects traffic in these parts to increase, es-

pecially in the 1939 Hupp Skylark and 1940-41 Graham Hollywood lines since they were built from modified dies of the coffin-nose Cord.

With the oldest parts on hand those for a 1920 Hupmobile and 1926 Auburn, some that are otherwise unobtainable are made up on standing contracts with manufacturers and machine shops. Among these are the high-mortality bevel gears in superchargers, heavy-duty wheels necessary to withstand stresses of cornering imposed by front-drive, aluminum cylinder heads and the universal joints used to transmit power from the Cord transmission. About 200 of the latter, made by Bendix, one of the original suppliers, are sold yearly at an average of $50 each.

All body parts, if anything more than a speck of rust, are salvaged with the sheet metal shop rebuilding doors, hoods, fenders, trunk lids and bumpers. The one item impossible to replace is the amazingly simple-in-design ventilated Cord hub caps. A-C-D substitutes a nominally-priced plain one but purists have paid other owners $100 for four of the originals that needed straightening and rechroming!

A-C-D folk long have been conditioned to expect anything from customers who arrive with a wild gleam in their eyes, checkbooks in hand and what appears to be a fugitive from the junkyard in tow. The British Navy captain's transatlantic phone call of a few years ago to order parts for his L-29 failed to raised an eyebrow and work went on as usual while the California cutie disrespectfully exposed her mink coat to grease and grime as she hovered over her Speedster all during its rebirth in 1951.

There have been touches of heartbreak too: an Ohioan put $300 worth of wrinkles in his restored Cord sedan 20 miles from the factory and other enthusiasts have indulged their passion for the classics beyond the realm of reason and their pocketbooks. One such was the realtor who was unable to meet the $3,200 tab and found no one interested in taking a mortgage when his car was complete; another was a Quebec magician whose sleight of hand at pulling surprises from a hat wasn't matched by his ability to discover cash in his pocket. Those cases are rare; when they occur, A-C-D sells the car and seldom loses. ●

GOLDSTEIN
1924 Stearns-Knight, though restored by owner W. W. Edwards, still can get parts at A-C-D.

A Murphy boat-tail version of America's great classic,

The Model J
DUESENBERG

CLASSIC CAR CONNOISSEURS have their special favorites, but whenever a poll is taken, the big model J Duesenberg always gets the most votes. This is the third Duesenberg to be featured in our Salon section, the first being Tyrone Power's convertible-phaeton, (November 1952), the second James Aiken's Rollston convertible (August, 1955).

No car, with the possible exception of the Rolls-Royce, has had so much misinformation·published about it. Some of the more amusing stories in this connection are contained in J. L. Elbert's book "Duesenberg . . . The Mightiest American Motor Car," by Post Publications of Arcadia, California. The Duesenberg was designed and built by the late brothers, Frederick and August, at their own factory in Indianapolis, Indiana (U.S.A.). They began building passenger cars there in 1921, pioneering such modern features as hydraulic brakes, a straight-8 engine, and an overhead camshaft. The big J model was sponsored by E. L. Cord (Auburn) and was introduced in December, 1928. It was truly a dream car designed to capture the interest of even the A to B driver with specifications and dimensions that almost defied the imagination in 1928.

In retrospect, the car had its shortcomings, as did any car of the same era. Some of the drawbacks appear in the later correspondence pages of British magazines—for example:

"The clutch has an annoying habit of breaking one of its vibration damper springs after about 20,000 miles, which sometimes makes clutching difficult, depending on whether or not the broken end gets caught in the plates. I am told that this has been corrected in later models" (after 1930).

Another correspondent wrote ". . . from personal experience of a number of fast runs under all conditions I rather doubt whether the engine delivered anything like 265 bhp. . . . The engine was in first class condition but the best acceleration figure obtained was 0-60 in 13.15 sec. . . . slightly hampered by a dragging clutch . . .

"Unfortunately, the chassis did not line up to this superb engine, being somewhat inclined to flex and never feeling quite right at speed . . . I shudder to think of the amount of bhp consumed in pushing these (headlights) through the atmosphere. The lights belied their appearance and produced a faint luminosity—that was about all."

"Summing up, this was a very interesting and in some respects magnificent car, but I certainly prefer my Speed Six Bentley for fast motoring with confidence."

The two commentaries agree with the writer's personal experience, and in an interview with two engineers from Auburn's road test department in 1937 both stated they much preferred to drive the supercharged Cord at 100 mph rather than the Duesenberg which had a tendency to tramp at high speed.

With respect to the claimed bhp figure of 265 at 4200 rpm, R & T printed an authentic factory power curve (May, 1953, page 33) which showed 208 bhp maximum at 3600 rpm. However, the performance data published at the time of the car's announcement indicates that the factory experimental car, at least, was develop-

Front end design avoids bulky look by tapered radiator shell and wavy bumper bar. Louvers are thermostatically controlled.

Cars now strive to resemble aircraft, but in 1930 the emphasis was on speedboats. Traditional Duesenberg tail lights are larger than some headlights. On this specially built, long-wheelbase model, the hood was widened 6 in. to give more leg room in driver's compartment.

Murphy body is all aluminum, with top of boat tail unpainted, polished metal.

ing an honest 240 to 250 bhp, and our estimated performance chart which appears on the next page is based on this data.

The car shown here is owned by John S. Lewis of San Francisco. It was built in 1930, one of five near-identical Murphy boat-tail speedsters, but this is the only one on the long 153.3" wheelbase. Other points of divergence include an extra long hood with doors instead of the usual curved louvers, a wider cowl section, and no cowl lights. (Compare with photo on the next page, which shows the short-wheelbase model.)

The engine number is J-120, chassis No. 2354, body No. 958, and the weight is stated to be 6040 lbs. The car was purchased from the original owner with only 7400 miles registered, and the only re-work required to date has been re-chroming the wire wheels and rear bumper. Special accessories of the period include an unusual turn indicator with tiny R and L lights under the left front headlight, an automatic cigarette lighter which drops a cigarette and lights it for you, a 3-speed electric windshield wiper with a separate motor for each blade, a yellow tinted glass windshield, a pair of dark green plate-glass visors and a spotlight.

The Duesenberg fuel tank holds 26 gallons and the owner gives fuel consumption rate as 9 mpg, although this goes to as high as 12 at cruising speeds of 50 to 60 mph. The three auxiliary tanks on the running board were originally provided to augment the car's cruising range on long, lonely western desert runs, carrying gas, oil, and water. At the present time the smallest of the three tanks still carries water, but the other two have been thoroughly cleaned and are used for scotch and bourbon.

While we prefer soda, the ultimate touch has obviously been overlooked. Where is the ice-bucket for champagne? ●

Straight-eight, dohc engine displaces 420 cu. in., develops a claimed 265 bhp. Special features include "Startix" automatic starter and engine-turned firewall.

COURTESY FRANK S. SPRING

1930 J DUESENBERG

DUESENBERG-J COUPE

SPECIFICATIONS	
List price (chassis)	$9500
Wheelbase, in.	142.5
Tread, f and r	60.0
Tire size, in.	7.00-19
Curb weight, (est.)	5000
distribution, %	50/50
Test weight	5300
Engine	st. 8, dohc
Bore & stroke	3.75 x 4.75
Displacement, cu in.	420
cu cm.	6885
Compression ratio	5.72
Horsepower	265
peaking speed	4200
equivalent mph	108
Torque, ft-lbs	374
peaking speed	2000
equivalent mph	51.2
Gear ratios, overall	
3rd	3.80
2nd	5.41
1st	9.46

PERFORMANCE, Mph	
Top speed, avg.	115.0
best run	116.0
2nd (5200)	95
1st (5200)	53
see chart for shift points	
Mileage range	7/14 mpg

ACCELERATION, Secs.	
0-30 mph	3.7
0-40 mph	4.9
0-50 mph	6.3
0-60 mph	8.6
0-70 mph	10.9
0-80 mph	13.0
0-90 mph	16.3
0-100 mph	20.0
standing start ¼ mile	16.3

TAPLEY DATA, Lbs/ton	
3rd	340 @ 50 mph
2nd	480 @ 40 mph
1st	off-scale
Total drag at 60 mph, 240 lbs.	

CALCULATED DATA	
Lbs/hp (test wt.)	20.0
Cu ft/ton mile	107.3
Engine revs/mile	2340
Piston travel, ft/mi.	1850
Mph @ 2500 fpm	81.0

SPEEDO ERROR	
Indicated	Actual
30 mph	30.0
60 mph	58.2
90 mph	87.0
118 mph	116.0

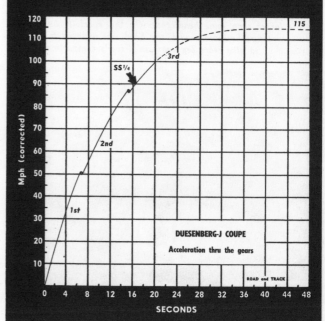

DUESENBERG-J COUPE
Acceleration thru the gears

ROAD and TRACK

Ed. Note: This test report is based on experience with (but not ownership of) two cars. The performance figures are estimated on the basis of data published at the time of the car's announcement and are believed to be somewhat better than the average car's capabilities. However, there are undoubtedly some individual cars which can equal or possibly exceed the accompanying data.

June, 1931: For sheer size, the current Duesenberg Model J must rank as the mightiest motor car built today, and its engineering detail is such that one's first impression is not belied by a detailed examination of the many features incorporated.

Perhaps the most startling aspect of this enormous automobile is the view under the hood. Here reposes a hirsute engine which fills all the cavernous compartment. With 420 cubic inches and dual overhead cams, the straight-8 unit is claimed to develop 265 bhp. Whether it actually develops this much is not too important—the real charm of the machine is its ability to pull at low speeds, a result of the conservative valve timing which enables the torque curve to peak at 374 ft-lbs at 2000 rpm. Even at 500 rpm the torque drops only to 335 ft-lbs, and this feature accounts for the ability to accelerate from 10 to 80 mph in high gear in only 22 seconds.

On the other hand, the engine is said to be capable of 5200 rpm in the gears, and this gives theoretical speeds of 52 and 95 mph in first and second. However, our test data is based on a rev limit of 4800 rpm, equivalent to a piston speed of 3800 fpm. High enough, we think. The transmission has close ratios and the internal gear design for 2nd is relatively quiet, enabling quick shifts to be made between 2nd and high with very little clash.

The steering, with 3½ turns lock to lock is near-perfect for the highway but rather heavy for city driving and extremely heavy for parking. Riding qualities are good, though no better than comparable cars.

Inevitably, with so large a machine powered by what is virtually a detuned racing engine, there are some drawbacks. The car is not particularly easy to drive. Except for the excellent vacuum boosted brakes the controls are all heavy, not perhaps "truck-like," but certainly too much for most women. Then, too, the engine pays for its high efficiency design by having considerably more mechanical noise than one expects from a car of this price. In addition the engine is quite rough when accelerating hard and the exhaust note is delightful or raucous, depending on the observer's viewpoint.

Briefly then, the Model J Duesenberg is a very large automobile, well built to give long life, and offering a performance which is not likely to be duplicated in lower-priced cars for another two decades. ●

This model, rather than the forerunner of today's convertible with a back seat, is most highly prized.

CORD 812

It combined glamour and goofs in a blaze of glory

AMERICA is known as the land of dull cars, but over the years there have been a few notable exceptions. Possibly the very last of these exceptions was the 1936-1937 Cord.

Errett Lobban Cord (now retired and living in Phoenix, Ariz.) had taken over the management of the sagging Auburn Automobile Company in the mid-twenties. By the time the Depression arrived, he had not only put the firm on solid ground—he also pulled it through the hard times with further gains. His success was attributed to 3 main assets, his earlier experience as an automobile salesman, his ability to interpret this experience and apply it to a product design which would sell, and an uncanny genius for organization in an era where tycoons were a dime a dozen.

Whenever E. L. Cord applied his talents to the automobile end of his growing empire, the results in terms of sales were successful. But, and unfortunately, Auburn, Cord and Duesenberg fortunes began to lag just at a time when other makes were beginning to rise. Whether this was due to neglect, as some reporters feel, is beside the point.

What happened is that the 2nd series Cord was the last brilliant gasp of a wounded company. In the summer of 1934, work began on a completely new front wheel drive car. Herbert C. Snow was V. P. in charge of engineering, and under his direction the chassis components took their cue from the newly introduced *traction avant* Citroen. The Lycoming division of the Cord Corporation came up with a compact V-8 engine, the Detroit Gear Company developed an all-indirect gearbox mounted forward of the front wheels, and

the crew at Auburn put it all together with the necessary adjuncts of suspension, brakes, etc.

The net result was a car with the wheelbase dropped to 125 in. as compared to 137.5 in. on the 1st series, model L-29 front wheel drive Cord. More importantly, the new 810 had 55% of its total weight (unloaded) on the front driving wheels instead of only 50%, as found on the L-29.

Engineering-wise alone, the 810 Cord was a radical but well-conceived development. But it was the sensational body styling which gave the car its immortal status. As is well known, full credit for this design goes to Gordon M. Buehrig, who is now with Ford.

In retrospect the coffin-nosed, venetian-louvred theme was little more than an automotive interpretation of the then relatively new cult of industrial design. But the idea was extremely effective and had adequate continuity. No one section or area looked at odds with another, and if engine cooling proved to be a problem (which it did) the design-for-function at least provided ample opportunities for air to enter and to leave the engine compartment.

The scarcity of both time and money which preceded the 810's announcement were responsible for numerous "bugs" which in many cases could scarcely be called minor. The over-heating problem has already been mentioned. The new gearbox also gave some trouble on the early deliveries.

In order to save space and thereby keep the wheelbase to a reasonable dimension the gearbox was completely forward of the front wheel centerline. Synchronizers for the 3 upper ratios required constant mesh gears and this, plus the fact that there was no direct drive, meant that a thorough lubricating system was essential. The early cars used an Archimedes screw-type oil pump that gave trouble. At high speed the gearbox oil would foam, and the pump would cease to supply oil. When this happened the reverse idler gear, which turns whenever the car moves, would seize on its shaft. Some of the company test drivers had narrow escapes as the front wheels suddenly locked up solid at 100 mph!

Other faults of the gearbox were a 1st gear that was best used somewhat gingerly and a complex electrically controlled, vacuum-actuated shifting mechanism which could hardly be described as completely reliable. Cord collectors have had special 1st speed gears made of a better alloy steel, with the tooth surfaces hardened by carburizing. Some have fitted a full manual shift control linkage rather than face the circuitry problems of the Electric Hand.

The ball-type constant velocity universal joints gave good service, considering the loads and angles (up to 37.5°) imposed upon them— and provided that lubrication was properly attended to and the oil seals were doing their job. The front wheel bearings were another matter, and a limiting factor. These were a standard (No. 5208) double row ball bearing, never intended to withstand the cornering style of a sports car driver. In truth, they gave trouble even at the hands of more normal slow-to-a-crawl-for-the-corner types and replacement every 10 or 20,000 miles was necessary depending on one's driving habits, with special reference to cornering enterprise.

Another shortcoming (which we hate to admit) was the widespread misuse and abuse of the 4 speed transmission. One true incident of this kind should suffice: The writer was one day (in 1936) offered a chance to ride for a few miles with a customer leaving the Auburn, Ind., factory. The owner was a nice elderly fellow, and quite proud of his Cord. We drove away in 2nd gear and once clear of the town the speedometer crept up to 60 mph. Suddenly the owner said "What's wrong? I can't seem to go any faster!" The tachometer stood at 4000 rpm at the time, when he suddenly remembered that

No bulging canvas here when the top is down. Not a trace remains when the metal cover is in place.

PHOTOGRAPHY: POOLE

Modern in its high level instruments, flush door for the gasoline filler and wheel design, the Cord is out of date in its poor vision.

Outstanding among the intricate dash panels of the classic period, Cord's included everything needed and some things not needed. Large crank at right, matched by one at left, wound headlights open.

he was still in 2nd. Further conversation, and miles, elicited the information that the 4 speeds were sheer nonsense (to him). He never used any gear except 2nd for starts and always shifted promptly into 4th at 10 or 15 mph! (He admitted that the car had been back at the factory for a new clutch.)

The V-8 engine for the Cord was designed especially for this car under the direction of F.S. Baster, then chief engineer of Lycoming at Williamsport, Pa., and now vice president and chief engineer of the White Motor Company. The bore and stroke were, coincidentally, identical to those of the 1937 Chevrolet, i.e., nearly square at 3.50 x 3.75 in. It was a good rugged design, with no unusual features except that the side-valve mechanism was reminiscent of G.M.'s earlier Viking (a 1929 V-8 by Oldsmobile) and the Oakland V-8 of 1930 (which later became the Pontiac). The valves were at a considerable angle to the cylinder bore axis, and pivoted rockers enabled the camshaft to be placed low in the V for a short timing drive chain. The angled valves gave a somewhat peculiar combustion chamber with a crowned piston which bore some resemblance to the shape found on the Packard Twelve.

The supercharger of the 812 model was mounted above a vertical shaft driven by gears off the camshaft. The blower itself was built by Switzer-Cummins of Indianapolis and had their patented planetary-roller step-up drive which was also employed by Auburn. The impeller ran at 6 times crankshaft speed, but despite this it was rather hard to distinguish by sound alone whether a given car was supercharged or not. Visually, of course, Cord followed the accepted trend (introduced much earlier by Mercedes) of associating flexible chrome-plated external exhaust pipes with supercharging. These were not at all necessary but in the case of the Cord, they undoubtedly helped to reduce underhood temperatures with an attendant increase in useful power output as well as providing some relief for the overtaxed radiator.

Incidentally, while on the subject of the powerplant, no torque figures were ever published, to the best of our knowledge. Accordingly the data which appear under that heading on page 29 must be considered an estimate. Also, as an interesting aside, the aluminum alloy cylinder heads gave some trouble (corrosion) and in later years replacements became impossible to find. A British firm (Aquaplane Co., Oulton Broad, Suffolk) can supply these parts, strange as it may seem.

Chassis-wise, the unique feature of the Cord was a frameless body to which a sort of sub-frame was attached at the cowl. The rather narrow body made it possible to telescope the sub-frame channel members into the substantial body sills, and 20 bolts completed the job. Armchair designers predicted dire results from this arrangement

but it appears to have been quite satisfactory, even on the roofless, convertible models.

Front suspension was of course independent, but it was unique in being a single trailing arm on each side. A single transverse leaf spring was used giving a rather high ride rate of 139 lb/in., measured at the wheel. At the rear a simple tubular axle gave very low unsprung weight and a pair of conventional semi-elliptic springs gave a ride rate of 120 lb/in.

The beautifully cared for convertible shown here is the special pride of its owner, retired Army Colonel Vincent Wilson of Pasadena, Calif. Several times, the owner tells us, he has considered selling her—and even set a price. But every time, he hopes it won't be sold—and so far it hasn't been, much to his relief. And who can blame him even if, as he admits, it would be nice to have a new 300 SL roadster? ●

Under the hood of a similar car, with its tiny air cleaner removed to ease the confusion around the V-8.

CORD 812

Ed. Note. This is another simulated road test in our Classic series. The actual performance figures were published in the book "The Classic Cord," by Post Publications. Most of the remarks are based on the Technical Editor's acquaintance with 2 Cord engineers.

JUNE 1937. It is hard to say anything unkind regarding an automobile so esthetically beautiful and so interesting mechanically as the supercharged Cord model 812 convertible coupe. The supercharged version of the Cord performs, in actuality, about as well as the speedometer of last year's 810 indicated. However, the error on this particular car was not as serious as found on the 1936 810, which averaged 10% fast.

Having said that much, we can now proceed to enthuse over this machine without further apology. With the horsepower increased from 125 to 170, the acceleration and top speed are well up.

As before, the remarkable close-ratio 4 speed gearbox with its Bendix fingertip control is a delight to use. First gear must be used for starting up, and it is a little noisy as compared to the other 3 ratios, which are satisfactorily quiet despite the absence of a direct drive. The shift pattern is cleverly contrived to induce the driver to operate the car as a normal 3 speed type, with 3rd gear in the usual high gear position. Since 3rd gear has a ratio of 3.88:1, it really is equivalent to a normal high gear: at the recommended rev limit of 4000 rpm it gives a road speed of 84 mph. The extra 4th gear (2.75) is engaged by moving the control to the right and forward, and being an extremely high ratio it is primarily suitable only for level road highway cruising. While no one with any appreciation of the mechanism would use this gear (virtually an overdrive, giving 29.7 mph/1000 rpm) at much below 50 mph, the large, relatively slow speed engine will accelerate the heavy car in 4th from as low as 10 mph. The powerplant is remarkably smooth and quiet and, if forced, it can approach 4500 rpm in the lower ratios. Also, overheating troubles with earlier models appear to have been overcome.

On the road, with front wheel drive and a slight weight bias on the driving wheels, the Cord runs straight and true with no effort or worry on the part of the driver. Corners can be taken very fast and a tendency for the front end to "plow" (understeer) can be completely eliminated by applying power. The steering has a strong caster return action and is free from road reaction yet has a good feel of the road. Steering effort is not light but requires only 3.8 turns lock to lock for a 41 ft turning circle.

In short, and from any viewpoint, the Cord is an experience which enthusiasts will find difficult to forget. ●

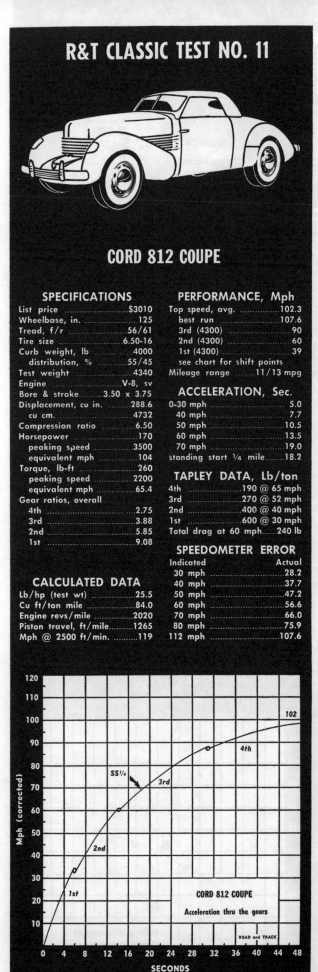

R&T CLASSIC TEST NO. 11

CORD 812 COUPE

SPECIFICATIONS

List price	$3010
Wheelbase, in.	125
Tread, f/r	56/61
Tire size	6.50-16
Curb weight, lb	4000
distribution, %	55/45
Test weight	4340
Engine	V-8, sv
Bore & stroke	3.50 x 3.75
Displacement, cu in.	288.6
cu cm.	4732
Compression ratio	6.50
Horsepower	170
peaking speed	3500
equivalent mph	104
Torque, lb-ft	260
peaking speed	2200
equivalent mph	65.4
Gear ratios, overall	
4th	2.75
3rd	3.88
2nd	5.85
1st	9.08

CALCULATED DATA

Lb/hp (test wt)	25.5
Cu ft/ton mile	84.0
Engine revs/mile	2020
Piston travel, ft/mile	1265
Mph @ 2500 ft/min.	119

PERFORMANCE, Mph

Top speed, avg.	102.3
best run	107.6
3rd (4300)	90
2nd (4300)	60
1st (4300)	39
see chart for shift points	
Mileage range	11/13 mpg

ACCELERATION, Sec.

0-30 mph	5.0
40 mph	7.7
50 mph	10.5
60 mph	13.5
70 mph	19.0
standing start ¼ mile	18.2

TAPLEY DATA, Lb/ton

4th	190 @ 65 mph
3rd	270 @ 52 mph
2nd	400 @ 40 mph
1st	600 @ 30 mph
Total drag at 60 mph	240 lb

SPEEDOMETER ERROR

Indicated	Actual
30 mph	28.2
40 mph	37.7
50 mph	47.2
60 mph	56.6
70 mph	66.0
80 mph	75.9
112 mph	107.6

Graph: Mph (corrected) vs SECONDS

CORD 812 COUPE
Acceleration thru the gears
ROAD and TRACK

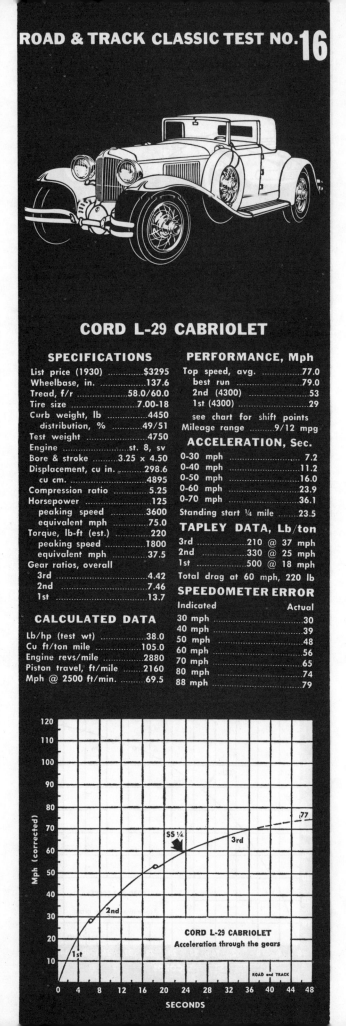

CORD L-29

Ed. Note: This is not an actual test on the car in question, but the data presented are an accurate synthesis of material published during the time the car was produced.

AUGUST, 1930. Not since the introduction of the Safety Stutz four years ago has there been such a new and interesting car as the front-wheel-drive Cord. Perhaps the unusual and very advanced styling has had something to do with the great interest in this car, but mechanically it offers even greater appeal to the enthusiast. Its front-drive feature alone, aside from being a notable pioneering effort, offers important advantages in road-holding, comfort and safety. However, we may as well admit at the outset that the car tested was disappointing in some ways.

In the first place, though the car is beautiful in appearance and exceptionally well made, it is not very easy to drive. The driver's position is good and all controls are well placed, although the near-vertical steering wheel feels a little strange and the push-pull shift control is not the easiest. Clutch action is smooth, and with first gear engaged one starts out. This gear is rather low and gives good fast getaway. Unfortunately the noise level is quite surprisingly high and the engine (which is smooth and quiet) runs out of revs very early. At first one feels inclined to shift from 1st to 2nd at about 15 or 20 miles per hour because of the gear howl, but if forced, the limit in 1st is about 29 mph. Second gear is also noisy: in traffic it is usual to shift into high at no more than 25 mph.

The gears can be selected quite quickly (once the control is mastered) with a slight pause going through neutral, then a firm, quick movement toward the next ratio. High gear gives wonderful flexibility, even down to a mere walking pace with the speedometer bumping zero. The big straight-8 engine will take full throttle at 10 mph in high gear—and accelerate brilliantly all the way to top speed.

However, here again we find objections. Anything over 60 mph gives a definite impression of engine fussiness, almost as if you had forgotten to shift out of 2nd gear. The test car had the standard 4.417 axle ratio. For our tastes at least, the optional ratio of 4.076 would be preferable, even though it would entail a little more use of the noisy indirect gears in traffic. The top speed proved to be an acceptable 88 mph, *indicated*, but the actual time recorded was a not-so-acceptable 79.0 mph. In a car which looks so fast, we felt rather ashamed of both the true timed speed and the extreme optimism of the speedometer. In this case one pays for the excellent high-gear capability (210 pounds per ton) by a considerable sacrifice in top speed as well as cruising speed. We would put the safe, comfortable-feeling cruising speed at about 56 mph (60, indicated) which is equivalent to 2700 rpm and a piston speed of 2000 feet per minute.

At all speeds the Cord handles beautifully. It is very low, which gives confidence, and with front/rear ride rates of 300/160 pounds per inch and exceptionally low unsprung weight, the ride is excellent. Steering feel is unusual, with considerable rim pull in a corner, yet virtually "dead" when traveling straight. The car seems exceptionally good, as compared to other types, on wet slippery roads. Curves can be taken under such conditions at really frightening speeds. However, we soon learned that it is best (if not absolutely essential) to approach a slippery curve at about the same speed as with any other car, then apply moderate power. This will pull you around somewhat faster than can be done safely in a rear-wheel-drive vehicle, though there is no r.w.d. car quite so long or low as the Cord with which to make fair comparisons.

Despite some advantages for f.w.d, as outlined above, (*continued on page 87*)

CORD L-29 CABRIOLET

SPECIFICATIONS

List price (1930)	$3295
Wheelbase, in.	137.6
Tread, f/r	58.0/60.0
Tire size	7.00-18
Curb weight, lb	4450
distribution, %	49/51
Test weight	4750
Engine	st. 8, sv
Bore & stroke	3.25 x 4.50
Displacement, cu in.	298.6
cu cm.	4895
Compression ratio	5.25
Horsepower	125
peaking speed	3600
equivalent mph	75.0
Torque, lb-ft (est.)	220
peaking speed	1800
equivalent mph	37.5
Gear ratios, overall	
3rd	4.42
2nd	7.46
1st	13.7

CALCULATED DATA

Lb/hp (test wt)	38.0
Cu ft/ton mile	105.0
Engine revs/mile	2880
Piston travel, ft/mile	2160
Mph @ 2500 ft/min.	69.5

PERFORMANCE, Mph

Top speed, avg.	77.0
best run	79.0
2nd (4300)	53
1st (4300)	29
see chart for shift points	
Mileage range	9/12 mpg

ACCELERATION, Sec.

0-30 mph	7.2
0-40 mph	11.2
0-50 mph	16.0
0-60 mph	23.9
0-70 mph	36.1
Standing start ¼ mile	23.5

TAPLEY DATA, Lb/ton

3rd	210 @ 37 mph
2nd	330 @ 25 mph
1st	500 @ 18 mph
Total drag at 60 mph, 220 lb	

SPEEDOMETER ERROR

Indicated	Actual
30 mph	30
40 mph	39
50 mph	48
60 mph	56
70 mph	65
80 mph	74
88 mph	79

CORD L-29 CABRIOLET
Acceleration through the gears

ROAD and TRACK

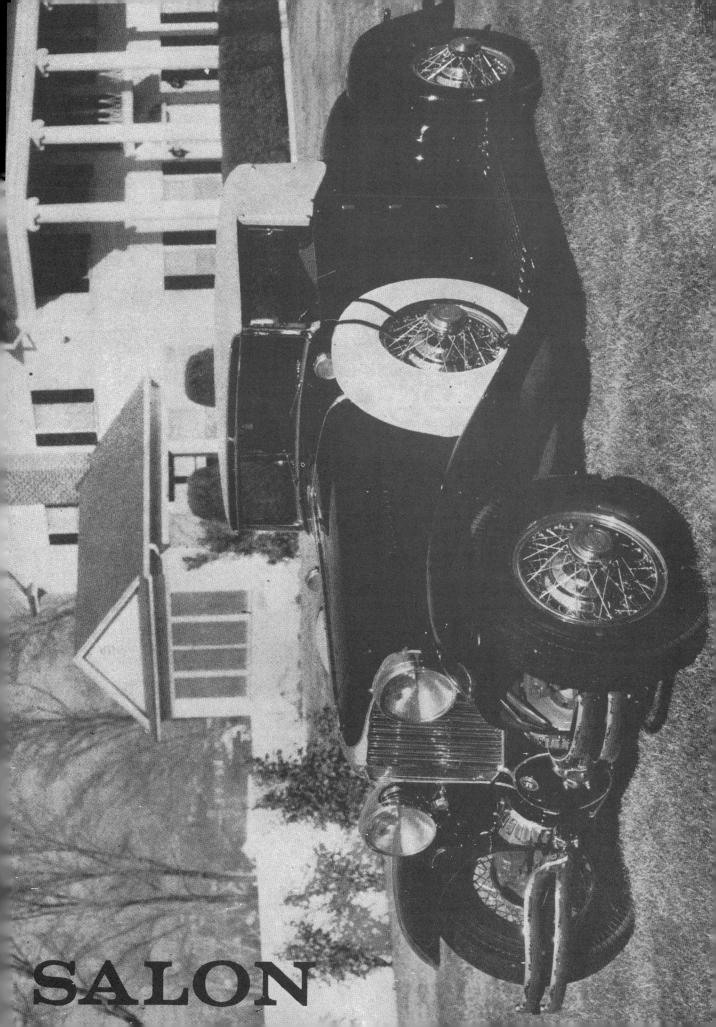

SALON

Powered by Lycoming

An outstanding classic
is this rare Murphy-bodied
Cord L-29 town car
on a 151½-inch wheelbase.
Compare this original front
end with that of
the restored cabriolet.

Cord L-29

In one respect only, it is the world's most important classic

BY JOHN R. BOND

E. L. CORD's December 1928 announcement of the 265-horsepower Model J Duesenberg was certainly sensational. Yet it must, in retrospect, be admitted that the L-29 Cord, announced a year later, had more significance. New Era Motors' Ruxton had scooped Cord by a month with the first American front-wheel-drive car; but it was the Cord's new styling theme that heralded what ultimately came to be known as the classic or "golden" age of motoring.

The Duesenberg was fantastic, but monstrous and very high priced. The Cord cost less than ¼ as much, and more importantly, it pioneered the extreme in the long, low look. It also inaugurated the sharp, V-shaped radiator shell. So successful was this styling technique (generally credited to John Oswald, who later went to GM) that nearly every manufacturer of every subsequent product in the world could be accused of plagiarism.

For example, an English motorcycle side-car manufacturer named William Lyons turned the conservative British automotive industry upside-down when, in 1931, he showed a long, low-slung coupe at the London Show. He called it the SS-I, and the car was a sensation. Amazingly enough, it was also a commercial success and founded a new marque—the Jaguar. And, let there be no mistake, the SS-I was (in appearance) nothing more than a British version of the L-29 Cord, with landau irons.

At home, other American firms quickly followed the styling lead set by the Cord. V-shaped radiator shells became commonplace, but the closest copier of all details was probably the 1931 Chrysler Imperial (Road & Track, May 1954). However, even the Imperial wasn't quite so long or quite so low as the Cord.

The L-29 Cord was long because the corporation built only straight-8's at their Lycoming Division and because, in 1929, the straight-8 had caught the fancy of the buying

public. The necessarily long hood was no disadvantage at all. Then too, E. L. Cord had put new life into the Auburn line by playing up big, powerful cars with long wheelbases: his Auburn 8-90 sport sedan, with a 125-inch wheelbase, sold for $1395.

The front-wheel-drive feature of the Cord is often and erroneously credited to Harry Miller. Actually Miller held a few patents which were purchased largely for what is known in patent law as nuisance value. The Cord f.w.d. design was the work of C. W. Van Ranst, and aside from the use of a de Dion-type axle it bore no resemblance to Miller's f.w.d. race cars.

The Lycoming engine used in the L-29 was identical to one used in the prior and concurrent Auburns, the 8-115 and 8-120. This engine was, according to some, the only good Lycoming 8 built, and certainly it had a far better reputation than the small-bore, long-stroke 8 ($2\frac{7}{8}$ x $4\frac{3}{4}$) used in the Auburn 8-90, the Gardner, Elcar, Kissel, etc. It was this "good" engine which alone gave the Stutz Blackhawk team such a real tussle at Atlantic City; an Auburn roadster averaged 91 miles per hour and finished fourth in the feature 100-mile "stock car" race. However, the 298-cubic-inch engine was not turned around for the Cord installation, as is often thought. Strangely enough, the flywheel was placed on an extended section of the normal front end of the crankshaft. This made the timing chain quite inaccessible. The L-head combustion chambers, at least, were the latest and best of the time; they were designed by R. N. Janeway for the highest possible ratio without roughness.

Though the engine was good (and proven) the transmission was something else. It was a conventional design, with sliding-spur gears and a direct drive for 3rd (high). Unfortunately, 1st and 2nd gears were noisy, and the final drive ratio chosen was eventually changed from 4.417 to

4.818 in order to improve high-gear performance and reduce the need for using the indirect gears.

Why cars with serious faults, such as the Cord, should be bathed in nostalgic nonsense is sometimes difficult to understand. Obviously the Cord could sell only on its appearance; the f.w.d. feature made good selling talk, but in 1930 and 1931 the few buyers of $3000 cars were not inclined to risk their money on new-fangled and untried ideas. Sales for 1929 were 799 units; for 1930, 1879; for 1931, 1416. Production of the L-29 ceased in 1932 after 335 more were registered.

Looking back, the L-29 Cord was a miserable automobile. It was far too heavy to perform, and the gearing meant that the salesman's claim of over 90 mph was utterly ridiculous.

The turning circle of 42 feet was inconvenient, and the outboard universal joints required constant maintenance, yet were very short lived. Any traffic accident worse than a minor clank meant very expensive repairs to the de Dion axle tube. Other than the above, the L-29 was a pretty good car—except that fuel consumption was atrocious (never better than 12 miles per gallon), depreciation was rapid, and it wasn't really a pleasant car to drive at all, either in town or on the highway.

The catalog depicted in great detail the advantages of putting the horse in front of the cart, but the public, apparently, still remembered the disadvantages of sitting immediately behind.

Two passengers per seat was about the comfortable limit. L-29's had true classic proportions: H=½L (H being the hood length, L the total car length). Below, the twin rear-mounted spares were rare on formal cars.

Eight-cylinder Lycoming L-head of the L-29 (used also in the 8-115 and 8-120 Auburns), was thought by many to be the only good Lycoming engine. As the photo shows, restoration was a painstaking one.

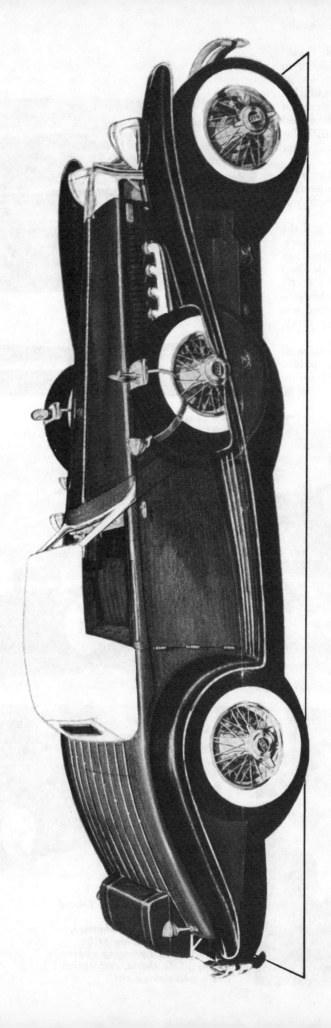

L-29 MEETS SPORTS CAR DESIGN

The Cord L-29 is a significant example of the radical classic. Its basic points—the long hood, V-shaped grille and front-wheel drive—give an impression of power and grace. Yet D. S. Bruce feels that the design's promise is unfulfilled. He has combined his 1930 cabriolet with a design by R. H. Gurr, which appeared in our Sports Car Design article of February 1955. The hood is copper-anodized aluminum, the body 1⅝-inch mahogany planking, the sweeping fenders fiberglass. Two leather suitcases form the trunk.

ILLUSTRATIONS BY D. S. BRUCE

Unseen improvements are the many power-assisting devices. The Chrysler power steering is particularly useful for removing the pure muscle factor from low-speed maneuvering and parking. Seats, top and windows have also received the power treatment, the original window cranks being very cleverly converted into switches for actuating the window lift mechanisms. Additional contributions to the overall luxury of the car are the modern heating and air-conditioning units. There is a back seat, usable only with the top up, that allows two more passengers to be carried. Overall height, with 16-inch wheels, is just over 54 inches. It is Bruce's intention to make the car suitable for everyday use. Though many of the classic automobile purists may mutter imprecations and abuse over the impending loss of another rare car, we feel that he has a very fine idea indeed.

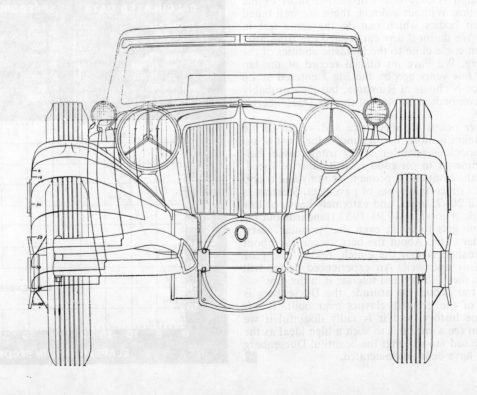

1938 DUESENBERG S-J

Ed. Note: This test report is based on familiarity with (but not ownership of) two cars, neither supercharged. The performance figures, therefore, are estimates but based on considerable experience in this area, plus correlation of a few published claims which appear possible though not too probable. Our classic test No. 4, on a J coupe, appeared in November 1956.

AUGUST 1940: Ever since our test on the fabulous Model J Duesenberg coupe a few years ago, we have been besieged by readers asking that we test the even more potent supercharged version, the S-J. Unfortunately, no such opportunity ever came our way—until recently.

The subject of this test is a long-wheelbase chassis. Despite the extra power of its supercharged engine, it has two strikes against it: 1) the test weight is 900 lb more, and 2) the axle ratio is 4.22:1, as against 3.80 in the earlier test coupe. The net result is that this car falls slightly below the performance of the earlier, lighter model both in acceleration and in maximum speeds.

The top speed, for example, is no better than 106 mph, 10 miles slower than the unsupercharged J of 1930. Even 106 mph meant turning the engine well beyond its power peak, actually 4600 rpm. Furthermore, the published claims of 129–130 mph could never be attained with any coachwork of normal frontal area, for the simple reason that 20% more bhp is not nearly enough to do the job (power required goes up as the *cube* of speed). Another claim which may have been true once can no longer be credited: the attainment of 102 mph in 2nd gear. Such a performance was possible at 5200 rpm when the transmission had the early-type gears, which gave a ratio of 1.29 in 2nd. Our test car (one of the last assembled in 1938) had a 1.42 2nd gear and could conceivably reach 85 mph at 5200 rpm in 2nd, but no one in his right mind would ever try it on such an expensive engine with such a long stroke (5200 rpm is equivalent to a piston speed of 4110 fpm, astronomical for such big reciprocating parts).

However, disillusionments aside, let there be no mistake about the performance of this magnificent machine: it goes exceedingly well, and its actual time of 22.5 sec from 0–100 mph is only one half-second short of the advertising claims. Without a doubt, there are well tuned S-J's with light bodies which can do the same test in under 20 sec. We doubt if any catalogued car from anywhere can even come close to the fantastic abilities of the S-J Duesenberg. We have no official record of the lap times made a few years ago by the Big J entered at Le Mans by Prince Nicholas of Rumania, but they probably were not too competitive in view of the big Duesenberg's unwieldiness.

On this latter point, the sheer size and weight of the Duesenberg makes it more than a handful for most of us. It requires meticulous attention at the front (wheel balance and alignment) to get good road holding at speed, and even then the front end is prone to shimmy and tramp at over 80 mph on certain types of pavement. Steering is very good from 20–75 mph, and extremely heavy at low speeds. The ride is good by 1930–1933 standards but far below what one gets today in even the "popular" cars, thanks to modern i.f.s. About the best we can say about driving this creation is that the clutch, brakes and gear lever work easily and well. An experienced driver will love the car on the highway and tolerate it in the city.

In spite of our debunking attitude, the Duesenberg is (or was) one of the greatest classics ever built. It has already become history, and it is sadly doubtful if we shall ever again see a car built to such a high ideal as the Big J. It is also sad (to us) that the beautiful Duesenberg radiator could have been so desecrated.

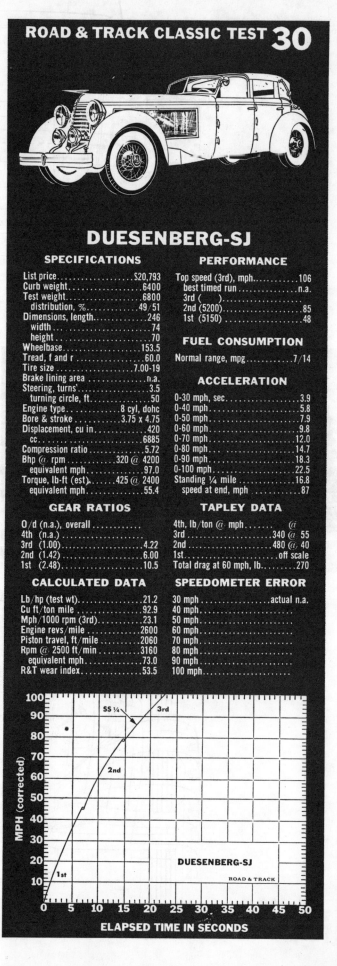

DUESENBERG-SJ

SPECIFICATIONS

List price	$20,793
Curb weight	6400
Test weight	6800
distribution, %	49/51
Dimensions, length	246
width	74
height	70
Wheelbase	153.5
Tread, f and r	60.0
Tire size	7.00-19
Brake lining area	n.a.
Steering, turns'	3.5
turning circle, ft	50
Engine type	8 cyl, dohc
Bore & stroke	3.75 x 4.75
Displacement, cu in	420
cc	6885
Compression ratio	5.72
Bhp @ rpm	320 @ 4200
equivalent mph	97.0
Torque, lb-ft (est)	425 @ 2400
equivalent mph	55.4

GEAR RATIOS

O/d (n.a.), overall	
4th (n.a.)	
3rd (1.00)	4.22
2nd (1.42)	6.00
1st (2.48)	10.5

CALCULATED DATA

Lb/hp (test wt)	21.2
Cu ft/ton mile	92.9
Mph/1000 rpm (3rd)	23.1
Engine revs/mile	2600
Piston travel, ft/mile	2060
Rpm @ 2500 ft/min	3160
equivalent mph	73.0
R&T wear index	53.5

PERFORMANCE

Top speed (3rd), mph	106
best timed run	n.a.
3rd ( )	
2nd (5200)	85
1st (5150)	48

FUEL CONSUMPTION

Normal range, mpg	7/14

ACCELERATION

0-30 mph, sec	3.9
0-40 mph	5.8
0-50 mph	7.9
0-60 mph	9.8
0-70 mph	12.0
0-80 mph	14.7
0-90 mph	18.3
0-100 mph	22.5
Standing ¼ mile	16.8
speed at end, mph	87

TAPLEY DATA

4th, lb/ton @ mph	@
3rd	340 @ 55
2nd	480 @ 40
1st	off scale
Total drag at 60 mph, lb	270

SPEEDOMETER ERROR

30 mph	actual n.a.
40 mph	
50 mph	
60 mph	
70 mph	
80 mph	
90 mph	
100 mph	

DUESENBERG-SJ

ROAD & TRACK

MPH (corrected) vs ELAPSED TIME IN SECONDS

SALON

THE 1938 DUESENBERG S-J

THIS 1938 DUESENBERG S-J is the last issue of an honored breed. Originally ordered in Germany by non-objective artist Rudolph Bauer, the chassis was finally built in the company's Chicago branch factory in 1938. The car is now owned by Bill Pettit of Natural Bridge, Va., and exhibited in his Museum of Motoring Memories.

The coachwork, designed by Bauer himself, was first intended for execution by Erdmann and Rossi of Berlin-Charlottenberg, but was actually undertaken by Rollson of New York. It was finished in 1940, three years after Duesenberg went out of business, thus becoming the last of their cars ever completed.

Rollson's original bill for coachwork came to $9043 and contained several noteworthy items: the special Marchal headlights, which cost $235; three black leather suitcases (custom made to fit the black leather trunk) at $225, and side screens for the hood, which listed at $175.

The body of the car is in excellent condition and car-

PHOTOS BY OZZIE LYONS

ries its superb appointments with authority. Violet is the color used throughout the interior—in the leather upholstery of both front and rear compartments, in the head lining, in the carpets, in the leather door paneling—and the turn indicator lens even repeats the color outside. The rear compartment has a sunken center section in the floor which contains two carpeted hassocks, also violet.

The rear compartment is separated from the front by the usual glass partition. A tasteful arrangement of ashtray, lighter and radio control lies before the rear passengers, as well as a buzzer with which one may genteelly alert the chauffeur.

At the disposition of the driver are all the gauges standard on a J (including an altimeter-barometer and a 150-mph speedometer), plus a pushbutton starter, cigarette lighter, turn indicator lights, twin ashtrays and a number of extra light switches. The dash lights number four, instead of the usual two. Tinted sun visors are made of glass, and are adjustable to almost any position. Full rear vision is assured by three mirrors, two of them mounted inside. A deep pocket is provided in each front door and in each kick panel, and most of the original tools are still under the front seat. A special air horn is supplied by a compressor mounted at the right front of the engine, powered by a pulley on the end of the lower horizontal shaft of the supercharger. A foot control operates the horn.

The body design is unusual even for a Duesenberg. A horizontal-barred, false V-grille hides the standard vertical radiator shutters. The bumpers carry three bars instead of the standard two and depart entirely from the Duesenberg double bow. The simplified hood spear is extra large. The most apparent design departure is the cycle fenders, which blend surprisingly well into this formal design. Craftsmanship of the top is, of course, excellent, and conversion of the rear portion requires only the barest minimum of effort.

Over-all length of the car is 20 ft 7 in. The standard S-J long-wheelbase chassis, 153.5 in. long, sold for a sturdy $11,750 without body. The total bill of $20,793 is rather staggering, but it paid for a great deal of almost priceless craftsmanship and prestige.

Duesenberg's mighty 320-hp supercharged engine carried the 1938 S-J to an advertised 130 mph, certainly adequate for the highways of its time or any other period. Complete technical data appear in the panel on the next page. The customary muffler bypass is intact, and must have had an all but lethal effect when called upon to vanquish lesser motorists of the day. But the last Duesenberg ever sold is silent today, for want of a radiator. The odometer total stands at only 10,368 miles, little over the break-in figure for an S-J but a strong contributing factor to the superb condition of our Salon car.

In its only showing outside the museum, the Pettit car was entered at the annual Old Dominion Meet at Waynesboro, Va., this spring. It not only scored first among the classics; it went on to take a trophy as Most Outstanding Car—at an antique car meet!

SALON

DUESENBERG

THE BIG DUESENBERG MODEL J, of all the great American classic cars, marked the high point of the roaring Twenties—a very large, truly magnificent automobile, engineered by the great Fred himself—with money no object, as the result of a *carte blanche* order from E. L. Cord.

The car shown here is actually a 1929 model J, equipped with the later type radiator shutters (as were nearly all '29's). However, we must also quickly point out to our readers that this car is not an SJ—the supercharged model was introduced in 1932 and the installation of SJ

1929 MODEL J

chrome plated external exhaust pipes does not necessarily mean that the engine is blown. These pipes were in fact a legitimate factory "extra," the extra charge being $927.75 according to the 1934 parts list. Likewise, the early cars had a dual updraft Schebler carburetor, but after November of 1932 a Stromberg downdraft unit was standardized and many earlier cars were converted to the later design. The "Duesenbird" radiator ornament was never standard equipment—it cost $25 extra.

Having established the year as 1929, the body of this car is a

Murphy phaeton on the short, 142.5-in. wheelbase chassis.

The performance of the Big-J has been well publicized, particularly the 89 mph in 2nd gear, 116 mph in high and 10 to 80 mph in 22 sec, in high gear (*Motor,* Dec. 1928). These figures appear to have been established by one of the first experimental cars, with a light 5-passenger touring body, and it is doubtful if any but a few exceptional or modified production J's could equal these figures (see R&T classic test, Nov. 1956). Nevertheless, the huge 420-cu-in. straight-8 engine, with its double overhead camshafts, had tremendous power and torque—more than double that of any car in 1929, and probably as much honest power at the flywheel as any modern car built today—despite claims of 325 to 375 bhp from certain V-8's.

Fred and Augie Duesenberg were solely responsible for the design and development of this mighty machine. Their planning began late in 1926, and the announcement came in December 1928, but no cars were delivered until the spring of 1929. At first, the orders poured in and

production was limited solely by the ability of body builders to supply them. As the depression came, and dragged on, the factory at Indianapolis gradually slowed down to an idle, then stopped completely in 1937.

An associate of the writer's who worked there during those dark days said that many of the later cars were actually assembled from odds and ends of parts and even from wrecked cars. This would account for the many strange discrepancies among the specifications mentioned in Elbert's book on the marque.

Fred Duesenberg was a designer and never very particular about the car he drove—any old experimental hack they happened to have handy would do. On July 2, 1932, while driving an SJ convertible coupe with (according to several accounts) smooth tires, he went off a slippery stretch of road on Ligonier mountain (in Pennsylvania). He appeared to be recovering from his injuries, but contracted pneumonia and died on July 22. He was only 55 years old at the time—loved and respected by all his acquaintances and associates.

August Duesenberg was the mechanical half of the

team—he built and made work what Fred had designed. He died about 3 years ago. So ended an era where cars were designed from bumper to bumper by one man—in the case of Duesenberg, by two brothers and a very small group of draftsmen. Since that day all production cars have been the products of very large engineering departments, which are governed in turn by management committees. The cars may be better, may satisfy more people, but they certainly lack character and individuality.

The restoration of our Salon car was carried out by Jack B. Nethercutt and crew in his immaculate shop in Sylmar, about 30 miles northwest of downtown Los Angeles. This is his second car to appear in our Salon feature section, the other being the virtually invincible (in concours) du Pont town car (R&T March 1959). Other cars in the Nethercutt collection are in the process of being restored, and all who have examined the caliber of the work being done in his shop can hardly believe their eyes—the cars are absolutely perfect and are being restored with an authenticity and a total disregard for cost most satisfying to the classic car enthusiast.

Auburn 852 Speedster

DRIVING AN AUBURN of any type is an experience not soon forgotten—at least in comparison to other cars of comparable vintage. These cars are big machines, nearly as large as several contemporary cars costing two to three times as much money. Yet, despite this bulk and concomitant weight, Auburns have always been noted for good acceleration and more than enough top speed. For example, any 8-cyl model built after 1927 would show very nearly 90 mph on the speedometer, and if this speed was not true velocity, it was at least a lot of mph per dollar.

The return of the Speedster to the Auburn line (in 1935) brought cheers from all the marque's supporters, and the addition of a Schwitzer-Cummins supercharger insured that enough power was available to propel this beautiful car at the speed which it appeared to be capable of attaining—that is, a genuine 100 mph.

Again, though the Speedster was tremendously heavy, the addition of synchromesh to the 3-speed transmission, plus a very ingenious dual-ratio rear axle, gave a combination of selective gear ratios more than adequate to get the best possible performance from the car. Thus, whereas former Auburns of this engine size had 4.90 or 5.10 axle ratios (and literally ran out of breath at terminal velocity), the Speedster got all the good acceleration of a 5.1 axle, yet had still another overdrive-type ratio (3.47) to provide lower rpm cruising and more top speed. Without the 2-speed axle, a ratio of 4.08 was standard—a good compromise, but one that took some of the fun out of driving the car.

The shipping weight of the 852 Speedster is listed as 3700 lb and we estimate the "wet" weight as 3850 lb at the curb. Add the standard 300 lb to that and we have 4150 lb for a test weight—equivalent to 27.7 lb per horsepower. Using four of the available six speeds forward, it should be possible to equal our estimate of zero to 60 in 15 sec, or a standing ¼ mile in 19.5 seconds.

Gearshifting is very easy, thanks to an efficient synchromesh on 2nd and 3rd, and the 2-speed axle shifts nearly as quickly, though the unusual hand movement to the center of the steering wheel seems somewhat awkward. Normally, the 2-speed axle is left in low up to at least 50 or 60 mph, and acceleration in this ratio (5.1) is exceptionally smooth and brisk—all the way up from as low a speed as 5 mph. The supercharger is quite unobtrusive in normal driving, but a faint whine or whistle can be noticed as the engine speed goes up into the higher ranges under full-throttle acceleration. The engine itself, like all straight eights, is notable for its low-speed flexibility and pulling power, and it is possible to pull away smoothly from 10 mph in the very high overdrive gear. At very high speeds the engine seems to be more fussy—a combination of mechanical noise, no air-intake silencer and a firm but polite bark from the bypass-type muffler.

The frames for the 1935-36 Auburns were stated to be 200% stiffer than the earlier types; and those were rugged. This fact undoubtedly was a prime factor in the excellent roadability of the 852. There is no trace of cowl shake at any speed and the steering is impeccable. Fast cornering can be indulged in without worry, although the rear end will chatter and break away on rough surfaces.

The ride is exceptionally good, thanks to such things as a long wheelbase with long springs, large section tires (7.00) and the previously mentioned rigid frame, which allows softer than normal spring rates.

While one owner we once talked with insisted that his Speedster had a Duesenberg head and an aluminum flywheel (ridiculous, of course), the fact remains that the 852 was a very remarkable car—if only because it is one of the few which attained "classic" status without being terribly expensive.

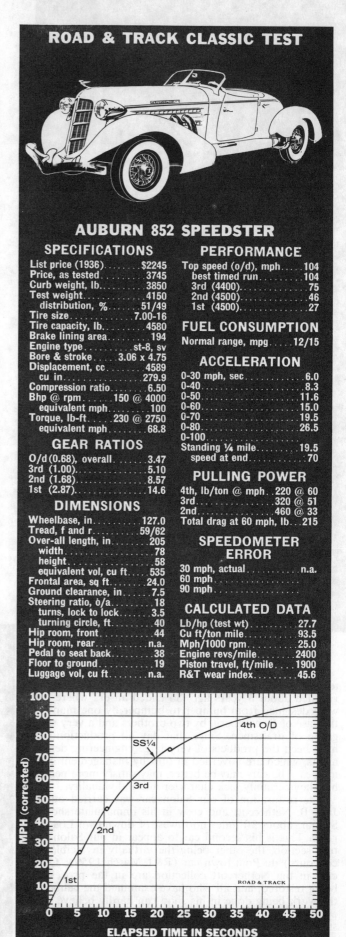

ROAD & TRACK CLASSIC TEST

AUBURN 852 SPEEDSTER

SPECIFICATIONS

List price (1936)	$2245
Price, as tested	3745
Curb weight, lb	3850
Test weight	4150
distribution, %	51/49
Tire size	7.00-16
Tire capacity, lb	4580
Brake lining area	194
Engine type	st-8, sv
Bore & stroke	3.06 x 4.75
Displacement, cc	4589
cu in	279.9
Compression ratio	6.50
Bhp @ rpm	150 @ 4000
equivalent mph	100
Torque, lb-ft	230 @ 2750
equivalent mph	68.8

GEAR RATIOS

O/d (0.68), overall	3.47
3rd (1.00)	5.10
2nd (1.68)	8.57
1st (2.87)	14.6

DIMENSIONS

Wheelbase, in	127.0
Tread, f and r	59/62
Over-all length, in	205
width	78
height	58
equivalent vol, cu ft	535
Frontal area, sq ft	24.0
Ground clearance, in	7.5
Steering ratio, ò/a	.18
turns, lock to lock	3.5
turning circle, ft	40
Hip room, front	44
Hip room, rear	n.a.
Pedal to seat back	38
Floor to ground	19
Luggage vol, cu ft	n.a.

PERFORMANCE

Top speed (o/d), mph	104
best timed run	104
3rd (4400)	75
2nd (4500)	46
1st (4500)	27

FUEL CONSUMPTION

Normal range, mpg	12/15

ACCELERATION

0-30 mph, sec	6.0
0-40	8.3
0-50	11.6
0-60	15.0
0-70	19.5
0-80	26.5
0-100	
Standing ¼ mile	19.5
speed at end	70

PULLING POWER

4th, lb/ton @ mph	220 @ 60
3rd	320 @ 51
2nd	460 @ 33
Total drag at 60 mph, lb	215

SPEEDOMETER ERROR

30 mph, actual	n.a.
60 mph	
90 mph	

CALCULATED DATA

Lb/hp (test wt)	27.7
Cu ft/ton mile	93.5
Mph/1000 rpm	25.0
Engine revs/mile	2400
Piston travel, ft/mile	1900
R&T wear index	45.6

Salon

AUBURN 852 SPEEDSTER

STORY BY WARREN W. FITZGERALD

PHOTOS BY SCHMIDT & FITZGERALD

IN THOSE YEARS between the wars, when the car in your life wasn't taken for granted as it is today, the raciest type of automobile a fellow could lay his hands on was a boat-tailed Speedster. Many firms produced them, and the names of Stutz, Duesenberg, Packard, Franklin and Auburn come to mind. The last flowering of this dashing style was seen in the 1936 Auburn Speedster, the supercharged model 852. After this the American motorist had to be content with roomier, more conventional convertibles and roadsters seating at least three people. The Speedster was strictly a two-passenger affair, an intimate, personal piece of romantic machinery . . . in short, the last of the "personal cars"—19 years before the first Thunderbird!

In 1934, a bad year for many people in the United States, the Auburn Automobile Company was in deep trouble. Founded in 1900, this old-line firm had been a competitive success, and as late as 1931 was in extremely good shape. However, in June of 1934 the directors of the company announced that for the first time since 1925, they had voted to omit the regular quarterly dividend of 50¢ per share. Auburn had gambled money on tooling

for the 1934 line, but the response from dealers and public alike was somewhat less than enthusiastic. Harold T. Ames, president of the affiliated Duesenberg company, was appointed executive vice president of Auburn, and assigned the task of coping with the serious decline in sales. In moving from Indianapolis to Auburn, he brought along the chief designer for Duesenberg, Gordon Buehrig. We asked Gordon, now with the Ford Motor Company, for some insight into the design of the Speedster. He graciously responded, and from his notes we can trace the story of its development.

It was felt that an inexpensive face-lift was the only way to stave off complete disaster. Further, Ames felt that adding a supercharged chassis with external pipes to the line would spark up its pallid sales appeal. He set Augie Duesenberg to work on the engineering. Ames was spending the Fourth of July weekend of 1934 at Lake Wawasee, in northern Indiana. He invited Buehrig to join him, and together they sketched out the proposed face-lift. The small budget restricted them to a rework of the radiator shell and hood. This was quickly translated into a full size clay model at Auburn and approved.

A "show-stopper" was needed, and a Speedster, missing from the Auburn line for 1934, was decided upon. They originally planned five such show cars. Down at the Union City Body Company there were a hundred or so bodies left over from the 1933 V-12 Speedster production, finished in prime and upholstered in muslin. One of these was shipped up to Auburn and mounted on a 1935 supercharged chassis. This narrow body required a new hood, so Buehrig designed one to mate the new '35 radiator shell to the '33 Speedster cowl.

The body was cut off just aft of the top compartment and a new tail designed in clay. Gordon relates that he would have liked to install a new instrument panel, similar to that in his later 810 Cord, but there simply wasn't enough money. Another economy measure was the mounting of one half of a radiator ornament on each side of the body, the Speedster's only special trim. Tear-drop fenders were made by stretching metal over hardwood forms, and required considerable finishing. Buehrig feels that had the company foreseen the demand for the Speedster, they could have cut its cost appreciably through conventional tooling.

The 851 Speedster was a hit at the automobile shows, and went into production in lots of 25. While contemporary journals listed their price at $2245, this figure is far short of the known delivered price. One, fully equipped except for a radio, was sold in Hartford, Conn., for $3745, tax and freight charges included. In all, about five hundred 851 and 852 Speedsters were sold.

Celebrities and sportsmen were attracted to the Speedster, and the resultant prestige helped Auburn for a while. Buehrig recalls that Walter Hagen, the famous golfer, demonstrating his typical flair for showmanship, would arrive at a tournament at the last possible moment and drive right out to the first tee. Dismounting, he'd take a club from his caddy and tee off, leaving his Speedster right there for all to admire.

Back in 1953, Thur Schmidt, then a northern Indiana manufacturer and painstaking classic restorer, decided he'd like to have a supercharged Speedster to share garage space with a 1933 V-12 Auburn Speedster he'd returned to immaculate condition. He traded a beautifully restored Auburn V-12 convertible sedan for an 852 owned by the founder of the Auburn-Cord-Duesenberg Club.

Never one to do things by halves, Schmidt had the Speedster dismantled, crated up the engine block and shipped it off to Detroit. There the Federal-Mogul Company installed new bronze backed bearings, line-bored it and planed all the mating surfaces perfectly parallel. In the meantime, the chassis and body were turned over to Roy Emmert, Schmidt's restoration chief and a master mechanic. Working with a crew of metal-working specialists, Schmidt saw the Speedster thoroughly redone with no regard for expense. When the car was completed early in 1955 it was likely the finest Auburn 852 Speedster in existence.

In the process of restoration, the engine was over-bored by about 0.090, and the aluminum head was milled. Schmidt relates that it would top 90 mph in 2nd gear with the dual ratio rear axle in high range. He never seriously timed the top speed, but in a series of short sprints checked with a stop watch against the odometer, it reached about 118 mph, and, even allowing for a certain amount of optimism, the car is probably faster than a standard production model, as it left the factory in 1936.

The Speedster isn't loaded with conveniences. The luggage space is tiny, and is accessible only from behind the seat or through a small hatch on the right side. Any baggage has to share space with the spare tire, removal of which requires wrestling it over a wooden "X" member in the tail. The handkerchief-sized top, small as it is, must be stowed by two determined people following a rigidly prescribed schedule of bow folding. Closing the cover over the collapsed top always results in minor chipping of the paint, no matter how much caution is exercised. All of these vagaries, however, can be forgotten by performing a simple ceremony: 1. Slide in behind the large black steering wheel and turn the ignition key in the

Oakes-Hershey-type coincidental switch and steering post lock; 2. pull out the choke; 3. depress the clutch pedal, shift into neutral, and leave the pedal down to reduce transmission gear drag; 4. depress the accelerator pedal and push the ignition switch from "OFF" to "STX." The resultant booming note from the Lycoming straight eight, with overtones of centrifugal blower whine, is enough to make even the stuffiest ignore the idiosyncrasies of the beast.

"STX" on the ignition switch stands for "Startix," one of the several interesting mechanical features of the 851-52 series. This device is mounted on the right side of the engine, and serves to crank up the starter automatically in the event the engine dies. Normal driving is done with the switch in the "STX" position. Moving the short lever through "OFF" to "IGN" will allow the ignition to be checked without kicking the engine over, and the car may be operated on this setting if automatic cranking is not desired.

The centrifugal supercharger is mounted on the left side of the crankcase, and runs at six times crankshaft speed through a combination of chain and frictional planetary drives. The factory claimed it capable of sustained operation at 24,000 rpm. Lubrication is supplied to the super-charger drive mechanism by a line from the engine. Obviously, any device designed to operate at such speeds requires very close tolerances, and it is true that as little

as 0.005 wear on any part of the planetary drive system would render the blower inoperable. Factory service bulletins enjoined against disassembling this system, and suggested disassembly of the lower gear case only when absolutely necessary. The bevel gears it contained were machined in pairs, and sold only in matched sets.

A Columbia model 800 A-5 dual ratio rear axle combines with a Warner Gear 3-speed transmission to provide 6 speeds forward. The Columbia shift control is located on the steering wheel hub and ratios can be pre-selected by turning the handle up for high, or down for low. Depressing the clutch pedal then allows manifold vacuum to effect the shift. Final drive ratios are 5.1:1 in low, and 3.47:1 in high. To avoid double calibration of the speedometer, its drive is taken off the rear axle.

The 150-horsepower Lycoming model GH engine, the supercharger, and the dual ratio rear axle made the Auburn Speedster a potent performer in 1935-36. Actually, only minor trim changes were made between the 851 of 1935 and the 852 of 1936. It is likely that most of the Speedsters were built with the 851 designation. Either Ab Jenkins or Wade Morton was supposed to have broken in and tested each Speedster, and a signed plaque on the instrument panel showed the top test speed attained—always just over 100 mph. However, there is considerable evidence from old Auburn employees that, owing to the time and cost, only a few random cars were actually so treated. At any rate, there is no doubt that the car would do an honest 100.

Jenkins took an 851 to Bonneville early in the summer of 1935, and smashed the existing records for unlimited and American stock class speeds. In a series of runs on the flats, he swept the boards clean in the categories from 1 to 3000 kilometers, and from 1 to 2000 miles; and set new class records for 1, 6, 12, and 24 hours running. Some of the speeds posted were: 104.393 mph average for the first five miles; 103.033 mph average for 500 miles; 103.695 mph average for one hour; 102.733 mph average for 1000 miles.

The dashing boat-tail and the powerful chassis graced with more conventional bodies only postponed the inevitable. It was announced late in 1936 that new Auburns were under development, and would be completed by February or March of 1937—but they never came.

Today an Auburn Speedster is a highly desirable piece of machinery. Thur Schmidt sold his in 1959, and the present owner, Paul A. Wilde, has a high regard for our Salon car. He might be persuaded to swap it for a classic in like condition which would provide more seating, but the fact that his investment far exceeds the original selling price of the Speedster bothers him not a whit. Most known Speedsters are restored and in the hands of loving owners —thirty-seven 851's and 852's are registered to members of the A-C-D Club.

Errett Lobban Cord's masterpiece, styled by Gordon Buehrig. This example is complete, accurate and absolutely original.

1937 CORD 812

STORY AND PHOTOS BY WARREN W. FITZGERALD

Y OUNG MEN UNBORN at the time of the 810/812-series Cord's introduction in the fall of 1935 are now moved by its beauty. Older men, whose teen-age ambitions were stirred by the sight of a Cord cruising effortlessly down an open highway, still yearn to acquire one. Despite the Cord's

The 812 wheel hubs. F.w.d. requires center-point steering.

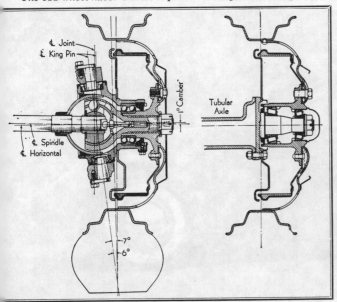

much-maligned mechanical frailties, this car is a gem among collector's items.

Gordon M. Buehrig was responsible for the body design of this Cord, for he initiated it and directed the small team which nurtured it through a period of frustrating stops and starts, all the while controlling its design. And in these circumstances can be found one sound reason for its success. In Buehrig's own words, "It wasn't designed by a committee— we were just trying to design the best car possible." Because the design of the Cord is the principal source of its veneration, and because it was the result of a personally directed effort on Gordon Buehrig's part, *Road & Track* asked him to recall just where and when the design concept began. The story starts in the summer of 1933:

The market for custom-designed and produced bodies on luxury chassis was all but wiped out by the Depression, but the value of well-designed mass production automobiles was becoming recognized. Under these circumstances, Buehrig decided to leave his post as Chief Designer for Duesenberg, Inc., and accept the offer of Howard O'Leary to rejoin the Art and Color Section of General Motors, as the GM Styling effort was then known. Shortly thereafter he was presented with a challenge. Harley Earl proposed a design contest among several teams of his artist-designers, with the idea that competition among them should create interesting results. The prize for this contest was to be an all-expense-paid trip to the Century of Progress Exposition in Chicago for the winning team. Buehrig's group consisted of five men, rather than the four allotted to other teams, because his people were newcomers. He wanted to hang his team's solution around some interesting theme, and being a lover of clean engines, decided that a hermetically sealed engine compartment would provide an excellent point of departure. Road dirt coming through the radiator core posed the greatest problem—but there was an answer. If the radiator were to be split symmetrically on either side of the hood between the fenders, only the hoses need be admitted to the engine room, and their points of entry could be effectively sealed. It would be nice to say that Buehrig's design won the contest. However, though it was acclaimed by his fellow designers, a jury led by the late William Knudsen and the brothers Fisher chose the design of a team led by Jack Morgan. Buehrig's twin external radiator idea was sidelined for a time.

In the fall of 1933 General Motors introduced a revised LaSalle, with its costly Cadillac components replaced by others in greater production. [Oldsmobile 8-cyl engine and chassis.—Ed.] The car's lines were handsome, and in fact initiated the tall, slim-nosed theme used by GM for the LaSalle until its demise in 1940. This junior prestige car, possessing more sales potential in a weakened market, caught the eye of Harold T. Ames, Buehrig's former boss and now President of Duesenberg, Inc. Impressed by this marketing idea, he called Buehrig, and invited him to spend a weekend at Indianapolis. There he outlined an interesting proposition. It was an offer to rehire Buehrig, and assign him the task of designing a "baby" Duesenberg, using off-the-shelf parts from Auburn production. Buehrig accepted.

On November 7, 1933, Buehrig drew two small pencil sketches to illustrate his ideas for the new project, and with them sold the concept to Ames. These two simple sketches were the only artwork ever done for the design which was eventually produced as the second front-wheel-drive Cord. Salient features of this initial concept were twin externally-mounted radiators between the fenders, and long horizontal fins low around the front of the hood. Also, no headlamps were visible.

The prototype which followed was built on an experimental chassis designed by August Duesenberg, and was powered by a Lycoming straight eight as used in the Auburn. Its lines reproduced Buehrig's original sketches with remarkable accuracy. The machine was completed late in the spring of 1934, but Buehrig's talents were needed elsewhere in the corporation. The 1934 Auburn had not been well received, and Gordon was put on a crash program to revitalize this car for the 1935 line. (See R&T, March 1961.)

When he finished this task, he was asked to go to Indianapolis and get the "baby" Duesenberg. He and Denny Duesenberg drove it back to Auburn. The project was in for drastic revisions. The car would now feature front wheel drive, and bear the name "Cord." The new version was developed in a quarter scale model by Buehrig, Dale Cosper,

The Cord's rear end was simple in design—bumpers show the evolution from bumperettes to full protection.

Dick Robertson, and Paul Laurenzen. Cosper affirms that extreme care and attention were paid to refining this model from the original. Buehrig recalls that they never felt that what they were doing would ever be acclaimed as classic design—they were just determined that it would be as good as they could possibly make it. When asked about the sometimes-criticized poor visibility to the rear, he replied that the then-limited curved glass technology dictated the small window in the very compound contour of the rear, a compromise accepted for form and streamlining.

Buehrig credits Bart Cotter, now with Fisher Body Division of GM, with doing a superlative job of translating the quarter scale clay model into full size body drafts, with no significant changes. By the end of 1934 the majority of body dies had been constructed. But Gordon was to leave the project for a second time—and for more romantic reasons. He married Miss Betty Whitten, and they left for their honeymoon.

He returned to find all work on the Cord at a standstill. Instead, some of the company management thought a cheap

The rear windows of the phaeton sedan could be removed, but did not roll down. Note that the front and rear fenders were not made from the same dies, as has been incorrectly stated.

One of the most beautiful instrument panel layouts ever used on an automobile. Note the fingertip gear control.

1937 CORD 812

Duesenberg was still the answer, and as a result of the impact of Buehrig's Auburn Speedster in the auto shows, a "Gentlemen's Speedster" Duesenberg, powered by a Lycoming V-12 from the 1933 Auburn series, was under development. About three of these hybrids were built, and one exists today. But this project was abandoned, as was another Auburn-bodied monster which was effectively damned by faint styling at the hands of a team of disgusted designers.

Suddenly the Cord project was "go," in space-age parlance, this time through the efforts of Roy Faulkner, President of Auburn. He sold the design to the board of directors with a series of photographs of the clay model. These were produced by Buehrig and Cosper in an all day-all night effort.

Original styling sketch for a small Duesenberg by Gordon Buehrig.

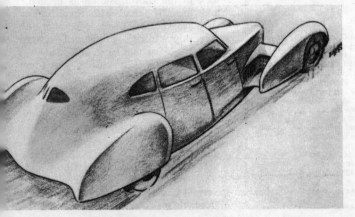

Just four short months remained until the New York Auto Show. Time enough indeed for one good prototype, but AMA requirements called for at least 100 production models. What happened is oft-told history, a tale of superhuman effort to make 100 hand-built cars, only to have the transmissions unfinished at showtime, precluding any chance for demonstrations. Six agonizing months were to pass before deliveries were made, and bugs still existent in the mechanical systems provided grist for competitive deprecation.

Still, the car which originated as a "cheap" Duesenberg captivated all who saw it at the auto shows. The first advertisement, itself a classic of its kind, showed the handsome snout of the prototype Cord emerging seductively from behind a rugged tree trunk. It was beautiful, as admirers a quarter century later affirm. But was there a worthwhile automobile under the glamor? The answer must be an unqualified yes. Because of the nearly unparalleled beauty of the Cord, we tend to neglect the engineering design involved. While this is understandable, the technical aspects of the car are worthy of similar respect.

The engineering effort expended on the Auburn, Cord and Duesenberg automobiles was a reflection of management's preoccupation with performance and innovation as sales stimuli. This type of engineering is of great interest to the enthusiast, but hardly the sort to be found in Chevies, Fords or Plymouths of the time. Thus, there were 265-bhp Duesenbergs, 160-bhp medium-priced Auburn V-12s, centrifugally-supercharged straight and "V" eights, front wheel drives, 2-speed rear axles, preselector gearboxes, and many other intriguing features. All these came from a fine group of engineers who never had enough time or money, and only the most meager test facilities.

The late Herbert C. Snow, who originated the "X" braced frame in American automobiles, was Vice-President in Charge of Engineering for the Auburn Automobile Company, builder of the Cord cars. His Chief Engineer was George Kublin, Ted Allen was Body Engineer, and Forest S. "Bill" Baster was Chief Engineer for Lycoming, builder of the engine. These four men held the prime responsibility for the engineering design of the 810/812 Cord. Assisting them were Bart Cotter, Chief Body Draftsman; William England and Joe Lavoie, Experimental Engineers; Stanley Menton, Manufacturing Engineer; George Ritts, Test Engineer; and Stanley Thomas, Development Engineer.

In the design of a front-wheel-drive layout, several courses of action are open. A principal objective is to bias the weight distribution toward the front axle, minimizing the effect of torque reaction under acceleration and weight transfer when climbing hills. Placement of the engine forward of the axle poses problems, such as excessive overhang, unless the powerplant is compact, as in the Austin-Morris 850. Placement of the engine over the front axle makes for high hood lines, unless flat, opposed engines are in order. The course selected by the Cord designers was to place the engine immediately aft of the front axle, attach the differential directly to the clutch housing, and go out to the transmission and back for the final drive. This arrangement resulted in a weight distribution of about 55% front, 45% rear, appreciably better than the 49/51 achieved on the prior L-29 Cord, which mounted a long straight eight engine behind a transmission, both aft of the front axle.

Front wheel travel was kept very close to vertical by i.f.s., utilizing a trailing arm and single transverse spring design. It was light and rugged, but the links between the trailing arms and the spring ends were known to break loose, and late models had "U" shaped keepers to prevent the end of the 34-in. leaf spring from clanging onto the pavement in the event of such a failure.

Rzeppa constant-velocity 4-ball universal joints were used on the 1936 Cords, but were replaced by 5-ball Bendix universals for the 1937 models. Eleven-inch-diameter hydraulic brakes were mounted outboard, relieving the universal joints

CORD 812 LYCOMING ENGINE

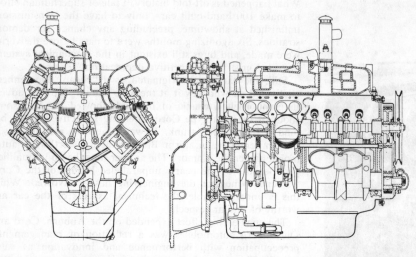

Cross section views of Lycoming V-8 engine. Rocker-operated valves and peculiar combustion chamber were similar to those of Oakland-Pontiac V-8. Note center camshaft journal, which projects far enough aft to provide pilot for mounting supercharger drive gear (not shown). Supercharged 812 engine appears below.

TECHNICAL SPECIFICATIONS: 1937 CORD 812 SC

Engine............Lycoming "FC," L-head	Transmission......Detroit-Gear 4-speed, Bendix-Electro-Vacuum shift
Crankshaft........3 main bearings, 2.50-in. dia.	
Cylinders..........8, 90° V	Transmission ratios.1st—2.111:1, 2nd—1.360:1, 3rd—0.903:1, 4th—0.639:1, Rev—2.533:1
Firing order........1L, 3L, 3R, 2L, 2R, 1R, 4L, 4R	
Bore & stroke......3.50 x 3.75	
Displacement......288.6 cu in.	Axle ratio.........4.70:1 (3.00:1 overall in 4th, early cars had 4.30 gears)
Cylinder heads.....Aluminum	
Compression ratio..6.32:1	Front suspension...I.f.s., single transverse semi-elliptic, 34.5 x 2.50
Brake horsepower...190 @ 4200 rpm	
Taxable horsepower.39.2	Rear suspension....54.5 x 2 semi-elliptics
Maximum torque...272 lb-ft @ 3000 rpm	Wheelbase.........125 in. (132 in. on Custom Beverlys and Berlines)
Carburetor........Stromberg duplex, 1.25-in. throat	
Supercharger.......Switzer-Cummins centrifugal; 4.5 psi	Tread.............56-in. front, 61-in. rear
	Tires.............6.50 x 16, six ply
Crankcase capacity..8 qt	Ground clearance...9 in., center of body
Coolant capacity...7 gal.	Battery............USL, 125 amp/hr, 6-volt
Fuel capacity.......21 gal.	Shipping weight....Phaeton sedan 3914 lb.
Fuel consumption...12 mpg	Factory list price...Phaeton sedan SC $3060

from braking torque. While this added to unsprung weight, it contributed to the useful life of the drive system. Actually, through the use of a light tubular axle in the rear and the engine-mounted differential in front, savings in unsprung weight amounted to 39% over conventional practice for a car of this size.

Engine, drive train, and suspension, practically all the mechanical components of the car, were mounted to a short stub frame forward of the firewall. Aft of this point, the body was built up around a "foundation" consisting of a cowl structure, floor, and rear wheelhouses. The welded assembly of this integral body-frame design contributed materially to its stiffness. Limited tooling money restricted the size of the stampings used in the body, and the roof, for example, was welded together from small flanged panels which required hand-finished soldered joints.

The transmission, which projected forward of the differential, was a Detroit-Gear 4-speed box, in which 4th gear acted as an overdrive. Effortless high-speed cruising was provided, and the supercharged model was turning only 2200 rpm at 60 mph in 4th. Particularly interesting from the driver's point of view was the preselector shift mechanism. A small cylindrical housing topped an arm on the right side of the steering post, and contained a finger-fitting miniature shift lever in a 4-speed-plus-reverse gate. Depressing the clutch pedal would effect the shift, but it was necessary to be careful not to release the clutch until the gear was engaged. This characteristic of the magnetically-selected, vacuum-operated gear changing system eliminated the possibility of fast shifts, and was responsible in many instances for some chipped gears. Actually, the transmission and shifting system were probably the weakest components of the car and gave rise to much of the Cord's reputation for mechanical frailty. As first produced, the Cord transmission had no provision for blocking inadvertent shifts into an improper gear. An interlock in the transmission was needed, and the "810 and 812 Engineering Changes" notebooks recorded that all cars shipped from Connersville after July 6, 1936 would be so equipped.

However, if fast shifting was precluded, fast driving was not. Good performance was a major design criterion, and in this area, the Cord shone. The unsupercharged 810 would top 92 mph, and post a 0–60 time of just over 20 seconds. The blown version, introduced two months after 812 production started in the fall of 1936, would reach 60 mph in just 13.2 seconds. Several seconds could have been pared from these acceleration times had snap

1937 CORD 812

shifts been possible. Top speed for the blown car probably ranged from 107 to 110 mph in standard trim.

The powerplants which produced this gratifying performance were the 288.6 cu. in. Lycoming "FB" and "FC" V-8s, which differed only in minor refinements, plus a supercharger for the latter. They were of fairly conventional flathead layout. Cylinder heads were aluminum, and the valves were actuated by roller rocker arms from a 5-bearing camshaft. The "FB" produced an advertised 125 bhp at 3500 rpm, but from the engine's very inception, supercharging was considered. The "FB" camshaft carried a shoulder at the center bearing to accept a ring gear for a blower drive upon future development. In mid-1936 that development started. A centrifugal supercharger, similar to that successfully employed on the 1935 Auburns, was designed by Louis Schwitzer for installation on the engine, which would be designated "FC." The blower nestled low on a special manifold, and was driven by a planetary friction step-up drive at 6 times crankshaft speed. About 4 pounds of boost was delivered at 4200 rpm, and 170 bhp resulted. Very shortly after introduction of the 812 SC, the blower ratio was increased to 6.5:1, boost was raised to 4.5 psi at 4200 rpm, and valve timing was modified. These later engines developed about 190 bhp.

Other changes from the "FB" engine were a heavier timing chain, a larger Stromberg duplex carburetor, a decrease in compression ratio from 6.5:1 to 6.32:1, and a change in firing order for better mixture distribution.

And the final touch was the addition of what became the hallmark of the blown engine in America, external exhaust pipes.

The Cord was a well engineered car. Had its designers been allowed time for testing comparable to that employed by manufacturers today, its mechanical quality would have matched its superlative appearance.

The 810 series was originally provided in three body styles: a 4-door sedan with two trim options, the Westchester and Beverly; a 2-passenger convertible coupe called the Sportsman;

and a 4-passenger convertible phaeton sedan. Actually, the latter was neither phaeton nor sedan, but rather a convertible victoria. And its rear window, which preceded popular adoption of this design by six years, did not roll down when the top was up, as is often written.

Interior room was rather spare, particularly for a 125-in.-wheelbase sedan, and in 1937 two stretched-out sedans of 132-in. wheelbase were added to the 812 line. These were designated Custom Beverly and Custom Berline. In addition, some highly individual cars were produced during the two years of Cord production. Perhaps as many as three hard-topped coupes were built, as were several speedsters. But likely the most curious of all were four cars noted in the records of engineering changes. They were referred to as "133.5-in. wheelbase Front Wheel Drive Cords with Duesenberg bodies!"

Our Salon car is a 1937 812 SC Phaeton Sedan from the collection of Russell Strauch, of Toledo, Ohio. It is without doubt one of the finest examples of the marque in existence today, and has garnered a roomful of trophies for its owner. Purchased in average condition, the Cord was completely disassembled and thoroughly redone. Strauch's insistence upon perfection caused the engine to be torn down three times. The original leather was removed, taken apart, recolored, resewn, and then replaced. Nothing was spared to make it as fine a restoration as was physically possible, a fitting fate for one of the most beautiful cars of all time. ◆

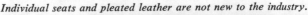

Individual seats and pleated leather are not new to the industry.

1933 Model J
DUESENBERG

STORY & PHOTOS BY F. ROBERT WOODWARD, JR.

O N A TYPICAL torrid Chicago afternoon in the summer of
1933 a 19-year-old college lad, heading toward Lake
Michigan for a swim, glanced into a Duesenberg showroom window on Michigan Boulevard. He stopped,
stared at an elegant, glistening Model J long-wheelbase Derham Tourster Duesenberg and, as Doctor C. H. Elsner of
Crete, Neb., recalls it today, never did get to the lake. "Instead," says the car-collecting optometrist, "I hung around
the Duesenberg dealer's shop, peering at the car and imagin-
ing myself at the wheel. I made a resolution that afternoon:
some day I would own and drive a Duesenberg."

In 1956, 23 years later, Elsner bought a Model J Derham

Tourster Duesenberg, and he stoutly maintains that it's the
same one he admired on that sultry Chicago afternoon in
1933. The history of Doc's Duesenberg is something of a
classic itself—with excitement, suspense, melodrama and, of
course, a happy ending.

In 1933 the chassis of Doc's car, with engine number J-504,
was fitted with a Gordon Buehrig-designed Derham Tourster
body. For its first two years the handsome green Tourster
was a factory demonstrator and showpiece, first in Chicago
and later in Los Angeles.

While based with the Los Angeles Duesenberg dealer in
1935, it came to the attention of a motoring sportsman

Dual driving lights, above, were a popular accessory. Instrument panel included a brake booster control.

named David Gray, who bought the handsome machine and kept it until 1950.

While using the Duesenberg for his private motoring needs, Gray made some alterations. In 1938 he installed the smaller 17-in. wheels, external exhaust system and Stromberg downdraft carburetor, all factory-approved options.

Recently, Doc Elsner received a telephone call from Gray, who asked the Nebraskan if he would sell the restored classic back to him "at any price." He was, of course, turned down. Gray had written to Elsner early in 1959: "We are so happy to learn that our old green Duesenberg is being cared for; why we sold it, we'll never know."

The man who first acquired the car from Gray was the late Charles Hoyt, who bought the machine in 1950 and took it to his home in Silverstone, Ore.

Mr. Hoyt, who was already quite elderly in 1950, maintained the car at his large Oregon home until 1955, when he finally agreed to sell it to Dort Lounsbury of Kirkland, Wash. It is from a letter Lounsbury wrote to Elsner in June of 1960, telling about the transaction, that a true appreciation of Hoyt's attachment to this grand old car is revealed.

"I purchased this car in 1955 from a very elderly gentleman in Oregon, who had partially lost his eyesight and therefore had been denied a driving license. I had heard there was such a car, and spent some weeks in tracing it. My first visit

with Hoyt and his wife started one morning around 10 or 11 A.M. We visited on the front porch until three in the afternoon, before which time he was not completely satisfied that I could be allowed to see the car, let alone purchase it. After his determination that I was not a hot-rodder or someone who would not appreciate such a car, away we went to a sagging barn, which looked nearly ready to fall down.

"We went through a few sections of the interior and into a partitioned corner, then to a bigger heap of blankets and quilts than I have ever seen. One by one, he tenderly removed them and there it was! I knew I must have this car, but money was of no interest to him. He was anxious to drive but, having no license, asked if I would."

Lounsbury's letter goes on to tell of a test drive out into the country with himself at the helm of the Duesenberg. Then, when in the country, "Hoyt motioned me to the side of the road, and said he would drive. Tears came to my eyes as I watched him put her through her paces. After a while, he pulled over to the side of the road and said, 'That's it, you take her. I shall never drive again.'"

After returning home, Hoyt asked Lounsbury to remain for dinner and spend the night as his house guest. The next morning Hoyt greeted Lounsbury by saying, "I want you to have my car. I feel she will have a good home. You can drive her away for $850."

Without a doubt, the greatest engine ever. The chrome-plated exhaust pipes and downdraft carburetor were authentic factory options.

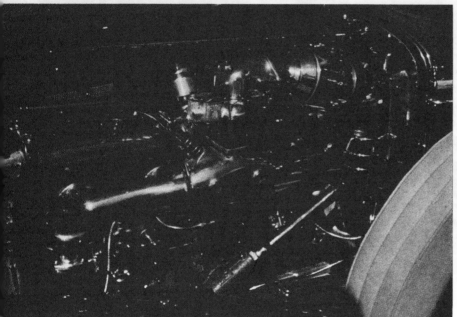

Leather spring covers were used to retain lubricant.

Huge filler was needed for 32-gallon tank.

1933 Model J
DUESENBERG

So, in spite of Lounsbury's protests that the price was far too low, the deal was closed and the elderly sportsman gave up his magnificent Duesenberg.

Lounsbury recalls, "He said the money was not really important, just so he knew the car was in good hands; he said never to let him see it again. I drove away that same day. Now both he and his wife have passed on. He was a grand old gentleman, and it truly made me sad to see his anguish when I drove out of his driveway."

Lounsbury states that he drove the car for 6500 miles of "carefree driving." In his letter to Elsner, he states that he had no major trouble with the car while he owned it. But by then the Duesenberg was without a top, and the chrome was deteriorating.

Within a year, "financial worries" caused Lounsbury to trade the Duesenberg even-up for a slightly used Jaguar coupe. The slightly shopworn Model J-504 became the property of a Mr. Henderson, about whom very little is known. Henderson kept the Duesenberg only a few months, selling the aging beauty to a man by the name of Fifield, who at that time lived in Denver, Colo.

Like the Duesenberg's original owner, Lounsbury later regretted selling the car. In a letter to Elsner he says, "I wish I could have kept the car . . . if I still had her, we would never, never part. If you ever get tired of the magnificent Duesenberg, let me know—I'll take her off your hands."

From what Elsner can find out, the machine did not fare too well while Fifield owned it. It is reported that the car was raced up Pikes Peak, the engine ruined and the car generally abused during this period. Shortly after selling the J-504 to Elsner in 1956, Fifield suffered a tragic death.

Elsner drove the car from Denver to his Crete, Neb., home on Christmas day, 1956, making the trip in spite of icy winter weather, which was doubly uncomfortable in the topless Duesenberg.

When Elsner got the vintage machine home and examined it, he saw that, in addition to the worn out engine, the once-beautiful Derham Tourster body was badly run down; its metal was scarred with dents, the chrome finish scaling, the upholstery tattered, and odd patches of paint had been indiscriminately daubed over various parts of the car.

In the fall of 1958, Elsner partially restored the Duesen-

The handsome trunk featured two hinged lids for complete access. Critics might call this over-restoration.

berg. He had acquired a blown J-392 engine, which he rebuilt and temporarily dropped into the weathered machine. This made the car driveable, and Doc was ready to begin the Duesenberg's restoration in earnest.

The original J-504 engine was rebuilt in every detail; larger valves were added, and cylinders were bored slightly oversize for new pistons.

In 1958 Elsner began a minute restoration process which shows no signs of ending and seems to become more elaborate each year. The leather upholstery (cream colored) has been redone twice. A new stainless steel exhaust system has been installed. Every assembly has been broken down into all of its component parts and refinished. Even the wheels were disassembled, spoke by spoke, before re-chroming.

The Doctor himself has been responsible for most of the restoration work on the Duesenberg. Spurning specialty shops, he has done most of the reconstruction in his handsome, elaborately equipped 2-car garage-cum-workshop. Elsner has even done some of the chrome work with his own homemade plating rig.

Although the Duesenberg has been returned to its original immaculate finish and is shown at every opportunity, Doc has steadfastly insisted on always driving the car wherever he takes it. The beautiful machine has never been trailered. This is one of Elsner's keenest fetishes. "A car like this was made

to be driven, not to be wrapped up and placed under glass," Doc says. Then the Doc will pause, wink and tell of the time that a Duesenberg took first place with 100 points at a show he attended. However, when the owner attempted to drive the car a mere 20 miles, the transmission fell apart.

Doc drives his Duesenberg to every show, every display and every concours. And, despite his having had to drive through violent thunderstorms at times, the Duesenberg has captured best of show in every contest it has entered.

Elsner believes the speedometer on the elegant machine is past the 100,000 mile mark. That being so, the total mileage is approaching 150,000.

Elsner has not limited his attentions to this one car. His stable numbers 15, consisting of all shapes and kinds, and ranging from hot rods to antiques. He briefly owned the Gary Cooper Derham Tourster Duesenberg. Parked next to his proud green Derham Tourster is a bright red 1935 S/C Auburn Speedster, which he sometimes uses as a tow car!

Within a few months Doc expects to take delivery of another Duesenberg. This, he has often said, he would like to make into "a fun car." However, upon sober reflection, he confides, "I'd like to fix my new Duesenberg up as strictly a pleasure car. I'm putting a hot engine in it. But I'm afraid it will end up being just like the Derham Tourster." Doc's friends think so, too.

The Unforgettables:
AUBURN · CORD · DUESENBERG

STORY & PHOTOS BY WARREN FITZGERALD

I WENT TO Auburn, Ind., a few weeks ago at the request of the Editor, who thought there might be a story in the annual meeting of the Auburn-Cord-Duesenberg Club. There was. I intended to begin by telling of the sleepy little Indiana town which comes to life once each year when the automotive ghosts out of its past come rolling back to town on 19-in. wheels, accompanied by the boom of robust exhaust notes rumbling down huge tail pipes. But it isn't quite that way. It seemed so when I last visited Auburn, three years ago. Today the town, riding along with the wave of national prosperity, seems brighter and livelier than I had remembered it. To the Midwesterner, the look of Auburn still conjures up memories of ice cream socials on church lawns, or mornings with the sound of horse-drawn milk wagons clopping along under the arched elms which shade most of the streets. To some local inhabitants, the sounds recalled are those of Auburns and Cords rolling out of the plant on the west side of town, en route to test runs or delivery.

The actual story lies in the A-C-D Club itself, for here is assembled one of the most informal, relaxed groups of automobile enthusiasts I've yet to encounter. This is not to say that factions haven't arisen. The Duesenberg boys, the Cord boys, and the growing bunch of Auburn boys all hold forth about the merits of their respective marques with no little partisanship. But farmers and factory workers compare problems with doctors and college professors in a shirt sleeve atmosphere so Midwestern that it is nearly a stereotype. The A-C-D Club was founded in 1952 by Harry Denhard, of Greenville, N.Y. It had as an aim, the ". . . restoration and preservation of three of America's most advanced and outstanding motor cars—Auburn, Cord and Duesenberg." And this 9th reunion meet brought together some of the most exciting and dramatic examples of these cars one could hope to see.

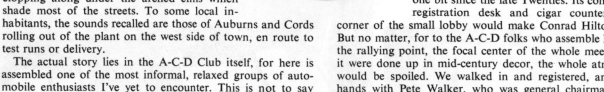

A friend and I drove in Friday evening, and found that the participants had been assembling all afternoon, with the Auburn Hotel on the northwest corner of the town square as the registration point. The hotel is one of the buildings in town which doesn't seem to have changed one bit since the late Twenties. Its combination registration desk and cigar counter in the small lobby would make Conrad Hilton wince. But no matter, for to the A-C-D folks who assemble here, it is the rallying point, the focal center of the whole meet. And if it were done up in mid-century decor, the whole atmosphere would be spoiled. We walked in and registered, and shook hands with Pete Walker, who was general chairman of the event.

The street adjacent to the hotel was blocked off by yellow saw horses, and behind these barriers the cars began to collect.

An impressive row of Auburns and Cords lined up on the football field for public display.

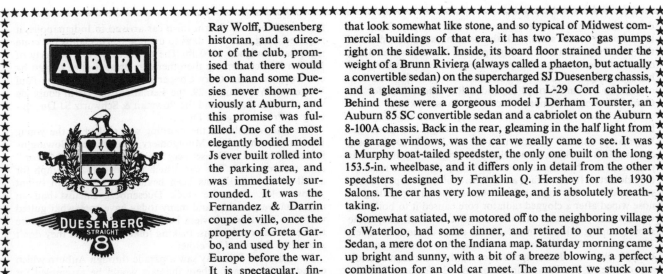

★★

Ray Wolff, Duesenberg historian, and a director of the club, promised that there would be on hand some Duesies never shown previously at Auburn, and this promise was fulfilled. One of the most elegantly bodied model Js ever built rolled into the parking area, and was immediately surrounded. It was the Fernandez & Darrin coupe de ville, once the property of Greta Garbo, and used by her in Europe before the war. It is spectacular, finished in gleaming wine red with contrasting natural canvas top and covered trunk. Inside, the upholstery is a very soft lemon yellow. Even the most knowledgeable Duesenberg buffs were slack-jawed. We wandered among the Cords and Auburns, renewing old acquaintances with owners and cars alike, and someone suggested we take a look at the Murphy bodied Duesenberg speedster over in the Chrysler garage. We did, and we got more than we bargained for.

Russell "Hi" Holden, proprietor of the agency, clears out all his contemporary cars to provide space for some of the well restored classics whose owners are understandably reluctant to leave them out overnight. His garage itself seems to be right out of the Twenties. Built of the cast concrete blocks that look somewhat like stone, and so typical of Midwest commercial buildings of that era, it has two Texaco gas pumps right on the sidewalk. Inside, its board floor strained under the weight of a Brunn Riviera (always called a phaeton, but actually a convertible sedan) on the supercharged SJ Duesenberg chassis, and a gleaming silver and blood red L-29 Cord cabriolet. Behind these were a gorgeous model J Derham Tourster, an Auburn 85 SC convertible sedan and a cabriolet on the Auburn 8-100A chassis. Back in the rear, gleaming in the half light from the garage windows, was the car we really came to see. It was a Murphy boat-tailed speedster, the only one built on the long 153.5-in. wheelbase, and it differs only in detail from the other speedsters designed by Franklin Q. Hershey for the 1930 Salons. The car has very low mileage, and is absolutely breathtaking.

Somewhat satiated, we motored off to the neighboring village of Waterloo, had some dinner, and retired to our motel at Sedan, a mere dot on the Indiana map. Saturday morning came up bright and sunny, with a bit of a breeze blowing, a perfect combination for an old car meet. The moment we stuck our heads out of the door, we could see we'd require a bit of time getting away from the motel. As there is but one hotel in Auburn, and no motels, the countryside hostelries collect the classics in clumps, and we had our share. There were two L-29s, two Auburn convertible sedans and an 812 SC Cord phaeton with us, and we' had to look them over.

Back at the Auburn Hotel more cars were beginning to gather, and stealing attention from the big red Duesenberg was the little red 8/10 Cord, as John Bond is wont to call it. Glenn Pray, president of the company which will produce it, was besieged by questioners, and a father with a new baby could not have been more proud. This prototype is well turned out, and the skeptics who prophesied that it would never see the light of day are somewhat confounded. Some diehards still

★★

Bill Harrah's SJ Speedster and Royce Kershaw's J phaeton.

George Templeton's 1920 Auburn "Beauty Six" 639L Touring.

McCord Purdy's 1927 Auburn roadster.

doubt that they'll ever see more than the first one. They fail to reckon, it would seem, with the determination and drive of this man Pray. His car is stirring up much interest, is well done, appears to be economical to produce in limited quantities, and has the weight of U.S. Rubber behind it as well. This firm makes the vacuum formed expanded Royalite bodies for the Cord Automobile Company, located in Tulsa, Okla.

More heads turned as Jim Edwards, Harrah's roving ambassador of good will, rolled up in the huge two passenger Weymann "fish-tail" speedster on the 153.5-in. SJ Duesenberg chassis. This machine, in unbelievable original condition, was purchased for the Reno museum with only some 1200 miles on the odometer. It was in fact, a stablemate of the Murphy speedster we'd seen the night before. Across the street, getting its nose wiped after a clogged radiator core caused it to boil over, was another Weymann car, the one-off L-29 Cord coupe, the show stopping Salon car made for the debut of the L-29 series. This low, very Continental looking coupe has a leather covered body, built in the Indianapolis shop of the American subsidiary of the C. T. Weymann Company. It features brilliant chrome wheel discs, and the unusual Woodlite headlamps in vogue for sporty machines of the late Twenties. The car was once owned by Paul Whiteman, the car loving father of the modern dance band.

Two local types walked up to the front of a gleaming Cord, and one asked the other, "Don't them look familiar?" "Sure do," was the reply. "Used to work on 'em myself." One fellow who once worked for Duesenberg, Karl Killorin, of Andover, Mass., arrived quite red in the face from a sunny 900-mi drive in an unrestored Model A Duesenberg. This vintage 1923 machine was one produced by the brothers before their association with E. L. Cord. Killorin was most interesting, and had some tales to tell. He had delivered at least one of the cars at the meet when it was new, and also recalled that when the body

for the Hibbard & Darrin town car arrived in Indianapolis, it required a big crew two days to uncrate it. He claims the crate must have weighed 5000 lb. The car became the property of Marion Davies. Among the other cars present once owned by celebrities were the Gary Cooper Derham Tourster, the Paul Whiteman Weymann L-29, the Fernandez & Darrin coupe de ville of Greta Garbo, and the Bowman & Schwartz SJ Duesenberg of Prince Serge M'Divani.

The relative calm of the morning was rocked as the young Kershaw brothers from Montgomery, Ala., came bellowing by in the ex-Ab Jenkins Duesenberg Special, or "Mormon Meteor," as it was renamed. This car, which recorded 152.145 mph for a full hour in 1935, has been beautifully restored in bright yellow color. Even the stock Duesenberg exhaust had an authoritative grumble, and many today have somewhat gutted mufflers. The Brunn Riviera boomed up Main Street en route to the parade rendezvous, making folks realize that they don't *sound* like they used to, either.

Noontime on Saturday saw a parade through Auburn which ended at the square, where the cars would be assembled for judging. The automobiles were preceded by the usual batch of Boy Scouts carrying flags, and the Auburn High School band.

As the cars were pulled into the diagonal parking spaces on two sides of the square, certain special examples were held out to be featured on Ft. Wayne television. Gordon M. Buehrig, who was able to attend briefly, was interviewed with the owners of some of the cars present. He then had to rush homeward, for his daughter was being married that very evening. Buehrig, in his capacity as body designer for Duesenberg, and later Chief of Styling for Auburn and Cord, is likely responsible for more individual examples of cars collected by enthusiasts today than any other living designer. And many of his creations were on hand at this meet.

The relaxed informality mentioned earlier was no more in

Edward Hedges' ex-Greta Garbo 1933 J Duesenberg Coupe de Ville.

Royce Kershaw's 1930 Murphy-bodied J Duesenberg dual-cowl phaeton

Vincent Furnas' ex-Paul Whiteman Weymann-bodied L-29 Cord.

Glenn Pray's Turbocharged Corvair-powered 1964 Cord.

Joe Kaufmann's ex-Marion Davies Duesenberg J town car.

evidence than during the judging of the cars which followed. Spectators swarmed around the cars, and the street was soon littered with yellow Verichrome boxes, popcorn bags, etc. Cameras were clicking at a prodigious rate, and the amount of money spent for film must have been astronomical. Competition did not seem so fierce at this meet as it gets at CCCA Grand Classics or AACA affairs. But among the top cars present there were some magnificent examples.

The Auburns, which often seem to take a back seat to the big Duesenbergs and glamorous Cords, were out in strength. One antique sedan was particularly interesting for its upswept belt treatment at the rear. Also intriguing was the 1934 convertible sedan, finished in that mustard-mayonnaise color the factory called "Cigarette Tan." This car was of interest, for the '34 models are extremely rare. They were designed by the late Al Leamy, but did not fare at all well in the market place. Looking back now, the convertible model, at least, did not seem bad. But it was a bit extreme, and admittedly, Buehrig's facelift for the 1935 851 models was a much more coherent design. This car displayed at Auburn had been a rotting hulk found in a field and pieced together from remains of several cars.

We waded through mobs of well fed farm girls and husky fellows walking with them, past the covey of kids climbing all over the cannon on the courthouse lawn, and found our car for the trip back and a shower before the chicken barbecue.

Eckhart Park, scene of the cookout, was filled to brimming with A-C-D members and their families. The American Legionnaire cooks had barbecue grills constructed from half 55 gallon drums set up on legs, and were broiling half chickens at a rapid pace. Even so, the lines were long, and we snitched a glass of draft beer and engaged in some serious car talk. Russ Strauch, whose prize winning 812 Cord was a R & T Salon car (Dec. 1962), allowed as how he liked tough judging by qualified men at these events. He felt that a fellow who had never restored a car shouldn't be a judge, and I had to agree. Russ is a particularly strong competitor, and his restorations rank among the best in the country. We finally got into line, got stuffed with barbecued chicken, more beer, and spent the rest of the evening discussing, of all things, the merits and idiosyncrasies of the Locomobile. This was started by sitting near Burles Hartline, owner of the Brunn Riviera Duesenberg, who had been towing his Locomobile behind the big SJ.

And that's about the story of the A-C-D Club's annual reunion for 1964. In retrospect, it was a whale of a meet. The Duesenbergs, numbering about 20, did much to make it so. These examples of what was America's most prestigious automobile, in contrast to the majority of Auburns and Cords, carried custom bodies. It is the opportunity to see some of these elegant and exciting designs that adds much to the impact. Ray Wolff deserves a lot of credit for exhorting owners to come out in force. Cars like the Weymann L-29 and the rare '34 Auburn convertible sedan add their own brand of spice. We drove back to Detroit feeling that any enthusiast within driving range of Auburn, Ind., would do well to attend the annual A-C-D Club reunion there next year.

Russell Strauch with Gordon Buehrig, chief stylist for the old Auburn and Cord companies. Below, a Weymann L-29 Cord and a 1934 850 Y Auburn.

Ed Zeugner, of Milwaukee, Wis. with his 1930 Auburn 8-95 Cabriolet.

Bill Kinsman's 1932 L-29 Cord.

The Kershaw brothers in the SJ Duesenberg "Mormon Meteor."

Phil Roger's 1932 Auburn 8-100A Cabriolet.

As our society gains in affluence, the amount of money men are willing to spend for desirable possessions becomes more and more amazing. We were impressed several years ago when a collector paid $12,000 for a not-too-well-restored Duesenberg dual cowl phaeton. Some time later when the original owner of a beautiful Duesenberg Derham Tourster offered to buy it back at the 1929 delivered price, something in excess of $16,500, we felt the cars were coming into their own as collector's items. Since then the price has been going up and up. Figures above $20,000 may seem beyond reason but they are being paid, a testament to the fact that the mighty Duesenberg, America's most uncompromising prestige car of all time, is a most sought-after possession.

The thought may be utter blasphemy to those who revere engineering accomplishment, but had not E. L. Cord been first and foremost a salesman, the well-heeled enthusiasts who now loose the floodgates of their bank accounts to buy old Duesenbergs would have to look elsewhere. Cord understood better than any of his contemporaries how to put emotional appeal into automobiles. He did a superb job, for that quality is still in his Auburns, Cords and Duesenbergs. More than anyone he established the strength of the "bigger-the-better" philosophy of marketing which has reigned in America for decades and is far from dead today. Cord also knew that *big power* had tremendous emotional value and to get it he purchased the services of Fred and August Duesenberg, two of the most talented empirical engineers in the country.

The legendary aspect of the Model J Duesenberg was created instantly in the fall of 1928 when the first Model J was shown at the Hotel Commodore Salon. Here was a car so clearly superior in every way to any domestic product that it defied the imagination. Against its rated 265 horsepower, the nearest competitor offered a puny 115. Its straight-8 dual-overhead-camshaft engine was frankly derived from the latest racing practice. It was offered with choices of wheelbase at an impressive 142.5 or 153.5 in. Its chassis carried no mundane factory bodies, but featured instead the custom wares of a distinguished list of American coachbuilders. The Model J was a deliberate attempt to captivate the most affluent members of our pre-Stock Market Crash society, and captivate them it did. The Duesenberg also became the cherished dream of a younger generation, many of whom were to fulfill their yearning by purchasing the cars nearly 40 years later.

Of the approximately 470 Model J Duesenbergs built, about 35 were the supercharged Model SJ, making these cars the rarest, most formidable and least available examples of the marque. One might well question the wisdom of "gilding the lily" by supercharging the already potent Model J engine. The answer is that shortly after the big Duesenberg's introduction its prestige was challenged by the multi-cylindered cars of such firms as Cadillac, Marmon and Packard, who were offering 12's and 16's in the rapidly diminishing luxury market. Duesenberg was in no position to retool for a new engine and because supercharging carried the image of super-power this was a logical way to go. Further, the Duesenberg brothers were well acquainted with the benefits of forced induction.

The supercharger is an American contribution to automotive technology and ranks with 4-wheel hydraulic brakes and the synchromesh transmission as a clearly domestic invention. The man responsible for this innovation was Lee S. Chadwick,

a Pennsylvania manufacturer of the cars bearing his name. Chadwick had built high quality 4-cyl cars since 1903, and in 1906 enlarged his engines by the simple expedient of assembling three of the cast-in-pairs blocks to a new crankcase. The resulting increase in power was not up to his expectations, for the new 6 was only 5 mph faster than the 4.

William E. Haupt of Chadwick's experimental department suggested the use of a blower to force the fuel/air mixture into the manifold at greater than atmospheric pressure. Chadwick's chief designer Nicholls laid out a simple centrifugal blower, belt-driven off the flywheel. The installation of this single-stage supercharger clearly demonstrated the effectiveness of forced induction. Later in the same year a 3-stage supercharger was developed and Chadwick's 1908 cars gave dramatic demonstrations of its advantages. The first public appearance and victory for a supercharged automobile came at the Giant's Despair Hill Climb near Wilkes-Barre on May 30, 1908, when a Chadwick Great Six won the event at record speed. That year Willie Haupt led for a number of laps in the Vanderbilt Cup Race until he was forced to retire with magneto trouble. Chadwick's cars acquitted themselves well throughout 1908 and 1909, establishing the supercharger as a method of obtaining very competitive power outputs in racing cars.

Curiously, little was done with the centrifugal blower in America or abroad until World War I, when the requirements for high altitude performance in bomber aircraft prompted another look at the device. Dr. Sanford Moss of the General Electric Laboratories conducted experiments with turbo-supercharged Liberty engines and in doing so became the ranking expert in the field. It was to this gentleman that the Duesenberg brothers turned in an attempt to get increased power for their Indianapolis cars. Dr. Moss' consultation, plus Fred Duesenberg's idea of using gears to drive the impeller, led to the installation of a supercharger on one car for 1920. The blower was 5 in. in diameter and though it imparted a screeching exhaust note to the engine, the car placed only 11th, indicating the need for much more development.

Centrifugal blowers, actually designed for Duesenberg by David Gregg of General Electric, were fitted to three of the 1924 Indianapolis entries. One car crashed, another sheared a blower drive pin and was retired, but the Joe Boyer/L. L. Corum-driven Duesenberg took the checkered flag, averaging 98.24 mph for the 500 mi. The following year found all of the Duesenberg entries equipped with centrifugal superchargers. Of the four cars, Pete De Paolo's was the fastest, winning at an average speed of 101.13 mph, the first to break the century mark. Another Duesenberg was 3rd at an average of 100.18 mph and yet another placed 8th. The supercharger had arrived and the Duesenberg brothers were its leading proponents. At the same time they were producing the Model A passenger car, itself developed from racing experience, and the heritage behind the Model SJ, some 7 years off, was becoming defined.

Though the Duesenberg brothers were triumphant on the track during 1924 and 1925, the business aspects of their passenger car efforts had been less than successful. The company, started in 1920 to build and market America's first production straight 8, had gone into receivership and was reorganized. E. L. Cord purchased the assets of the company in 1926, bringing together the ingredients of emotional appeal and engineering which were to culminate in the Models J and SJ. Assembly

1933 DUESENBERG

of Model A's continued through 1926 as design progressed on the new Model J. In 1927, 17 interim Model X Duesenbergs were built, powered by revised versions of the single overhead cam Model A engines, with larger chassis and bodies.

To any lover of things mechanical, the Model J Duesenberg engine is still a delight to behold. Long, polished aluminum covers for the dual overhead camshafts top the head and block castings, which are enameled a bright but pleasant green. Brilliant accents of aluminum occur where accessories are covered, and bits of brighter chromium are scattered about with mechanical logic. Inside the engine, the years of experience and knowledge accumulated by the brothers Duesenberg influenced the layout. A look at the transverse section reveals a classic racing design with straight-through porting. The valve train reflects Fred Duesenberg's meticulous detailing, particularly in the generous passages around the valves to insure adequate cooling. Two intake and two exhaust valves were provided for each cylinder. The cam lobes acted directly on cups attached to the valve stems and double valve springs were used. The combustion chambers, machined all over, held a single spark plug in the center of their domed roofs.

Ray-Day aluminum pistons were used with heat-treated dural connecting rods. With the advent of the SJ engine, the rods were changed to tubular steel and many earlier cars were converted. Throughout the design of components, painstaking attention to detail abounded. One example can be found in the rod bolts. Considerable heft was added to the big end of the rod by the use of a round head on the bolt, one side of which was contoured to bear against the rod, eliminating the

The Weymann Speedster photographed in 1933, and again in 1965 with designer Gordon Buehrig and Bill Harrah, in front of the Harrah Automobile Collection museum in Sparks (Reno), Nevada.

need for a conventional hex head. The use of a mercury-filled torsional vibration damper on the crankshaft was another example. Incipient vibration would cause the mercury to surge around baffles in a chamber, damping it before it developed. A full enumeration of the various ingenious and expensive technical features would exceed the scope of this article. Comprehensive coverage of the subject can be found in J. L. Elbert's *Duesenberg, Mightiest American Motor Car*, first published in 1949 and still the standard reference.

The engine was rated at 265 bhp @ 4200 rpm and the maximum torque was 374 lb-ft @ 2000 rpm, making the Model J a prime mover for its time. *Road & Track* has stated earlier that power curves from the 10th production engine show only 208 bhp @ 3600 rpm. Actually, the figures produced for the third test, engine J-110, show 213 bhp @ 3600 rpm and 380 lb-ft of torque @ 2000 rpm. More important is that J-110 was a *rejected* engine, which was disassembled and some of its components used in other engines. J-110 was never installed in a Duesenberg, and its crankshaft never appeared in any known engine.

Cradling the big powerplant was an equally massive frame. C-section side rails, 8.5 in. deep, were formed from 0.219 alloy steel and were connected by six tubular cross members. In keeping with the practice of the period, this frame was exceedingly stiff. Originally, four double-acting hydraulic shock absorbers were used but later the front units were replaced with Watson Stabilators. The late John Warren Watson, a close friend of Fred Duesenberg, was instrumental in solving an early poor ride problem incurred with the prototype J. He recommended the use of a soft spring rate at the front, which accounts for the many thin leaves found in the semi-elliptic springs. Hydraulic brakes on all four wheels, 15 in. diameter and 3 in. wide, provided stopping power for this heavy car. Late in 1929 a vacuum power booster was made standard.

William R. Beckman, chief engineer and draftsman for the Duesenberg brothers and the graduate engineer member of their small team, recalled that during the production of the Model A several experiments with supercharging were conducted. Running at 12,000 rpm, the blowers delivered a low boost of about 5-6 psi. They operated more as mechanical fuel mixers than as superchargers. It is apparent that Fred Duesenberg had a continuing interest in this area and that the decision to supercharge the Model J, coming late in 1931, had been in the back of his mind for some time.

Just when the first SJ took to the road is a matter of minor debate among historians of the marque. Records in the hands of Marshall Merkes, who bought the factory parts, documents and other assets of Duesenberg, Inc., when operations ceased, reveal that the first blower castings were delivered in mid-April of 1932. He feels that it was May before the prototype was ready. Jerry Gebby, who lives in Indianapolis and worked there at the time, says he was told by the late Shirley Mitchell, factory service representative, that the car was running in March. Gebby feels that the first blower was obtained informally, without paperwork, and that the purchase requisitions cover production parts.

In a May 14, 1932, article in *Automotive Industries* an increase of 20% in power was claimed for the prototype. 0-100 mph was said to have been reached in 17 sec, and 104 mph

was attained in 2nd gear. No top speed was announced. Supercharger details changed when the production SJs appeared were the impeller cover, water hook-up, and the Juhasz carburetor. The installation was mounted on the right side of the engine atop a tall vertical shaft driven from an accessory shaft below. A worm gear on the impeller shaft stepped up the drive to six times engine speed, resulting in 8 psi of boost at 4000 rpm. This was moderate pressurization and, rather than requiring cooling, called for water heating for even better vaporization of the mixture.

The supercharger shaft interfered with the normal Model J exhaust manifold and resulted in the development of the well known external exhaust system. The first seven SJs had 8-port single piece manifolds, gracefully formed and welded up out of Monel-like alloy pipe. Three of these seven SJs exist today. Subsequent SJs featured individual chromium flex-pipe headers off 2-port stub manifolds, which became the American symbol for supercharged cars. These installations became so popular that the factory offered them as extra cost options or conversions for any Model J. Thus, their appearance is no indication that a particular Duesenberg is supercharged.

Tragically, Fred Duesenberg did not live to see the SJ go into production. One rainy July night while returning from a visit to the New York factory sales branch he slid off the road on Ligonier Mountain in Pennsylvania. The accident is attributed to the prototype's being equipped with a set of old tires and wheels commonly used when driving cars back and forth to the test track. Fred's injuries did not appear to be critical, but he suffered a relapse and died on July 26, 1932.

His lifetime partner, brother Augie Duesenberg, carried on the development of the supercharger, and Walter Troemel executed the drawings and made many of the changes required

before putting it into production. No one can say just how many examples of the Model SJ were built but Marshall Merkes' records show that 36 superchargers were assembled. Of that total, 31 have been accounted for today, and one is unused, so a maximum of 35 SJs could have been assembled. The superchargers, apparently rushed into production with bugs remaining, were noisy and temperamental, causing many owners to disconnect them or have them removed by the factory. Others requested conversions of their cars to SJ specifications, and factory-rebuilt cars could have been equipped with used blowers. Over the years so many cars have been converted, unconverted and reconverted, that the SJ picture is quite obscure.

Our Salon car, a Weymann-bodied SJ, was created when Gordon Buehrig received a request from the sales department to design a speedster on the 153.5-in. chassis. If he had any conditions to meet he cannot recall them today, and he had no contact with the customer. The original design drawing, of which we have a print, shows the car equipped with the characteristic Duesenberg "bow-tie" bumper, but when the car was completed it carried the curvaceous Auburn type bumper. Buehrig finished the drawing, but did not see the actual car until recently when he visited Harrah's Automobile Collection, where the Weymann speedster now resides.

This Duesenberg, which likely vies with the Bugatti Royale roadster for the distinction of being the largest 2-passenger automobile built, was constructed by the Weymann American Body Co. of Indianapolis, to the order of Capt. George Whittell, a wealthy resident of Lake Tahoe and Woodside, Calif. He was an honorary fire marshal, and had a siren and emergency light installed by the factory. The car received little use because it caused quite a stir whenever it was parked

1933 DUESENBERG SJ SPECIFICATIONS

Engine: dohc straight-8, 5 main bearings, built by Lycoming to Duesenberg design
Bore x stroke, in/mm . .3.75 x 4.75/148 x 186
Displacement, cu in/cc 420/6885
Cylinder head: cast iron, 4 valves per cylinder
Supercharger: centrifugal, gear driven, 8 psi boost @ 4000 rpm
Compression ratio 5.2:1
Horsepower @ rpm . . . . .320 @ 4750
Torque, lb-ft @ rpm . . . . .blown n.a.
Unblown . . . . .374 @ 2000
Carburetor make . . . . .Stromberg
Crankcase capacity, qt 12
Coolant capacity, gal 8

Fuel capacity, gal 26.5
Transmission . . . . .Warner 3-speed
Gear ratios: 3rd 1.000:1
2nd 1.397:1
1st 2.485:1
Final drive ratios . . . .3.8, 4.1, 4.3 or 4.7:1
Frame: ladder type with 6 tubular cross members
Material . . . . .0.219 steel
Front suspension: semi-elliptics 41 x 2.5 in
Rear suspension: semi-elliptics 62 x 2.5 in
Wheelbase, in . . .142.5 or 153.5 (optional)
Track, front/rear 57.25/58.0
Tire size . . . . .7.00 x 19
Ground clearance, in 9.0
Battery . . . . Exide 160 amp/hr
Factory list price, approx $17,000

1933 DUESENBERG

at the curb and Capt. Whittell soon tired of elbowing his way through admiring spectators. The Weymann Speedster had only 1342 miles on the odometer when it was purchased for the Harrah collection. The car needed little but polishing to return it to mint condition.

Mr. Harrah has shipped the car all over the country for exhibition at historic car meets and it never fails to draw gasps of amazement. It is without any doubt one of the most impressive Duesenbergs assembled.

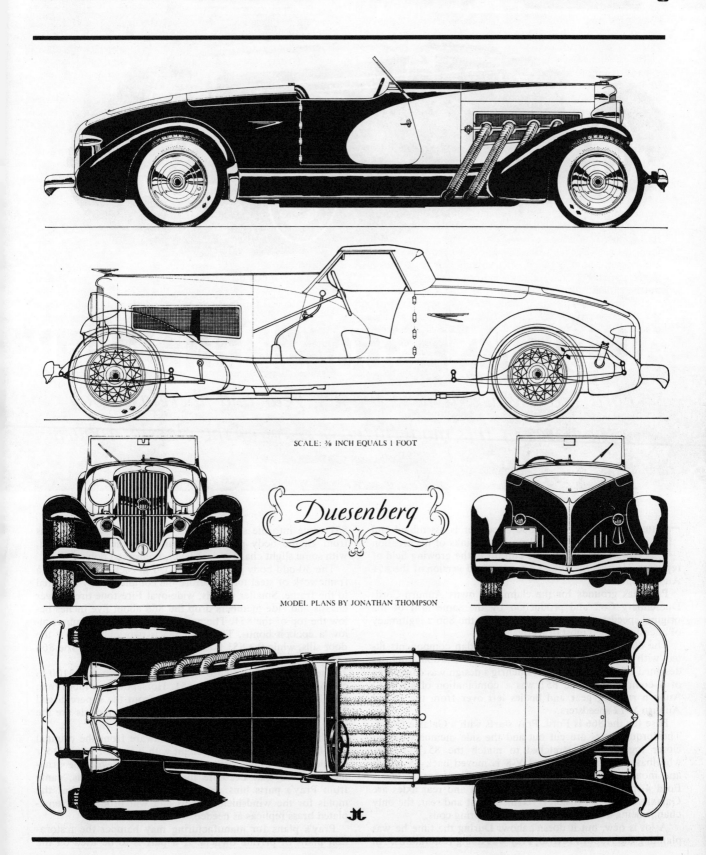

SCALE: ⅜ INCH EQUALS 1 FOOT

Duesenberg

MODEL PLANS BY JONATHAN THOMPSON

AUBURN 866 SPEEDSTER

*Ford 428 engine, Galaxie running gear and fiberglass body
are the bases of this modernized version of the classic Auburn*

BY ALLAN GIRDLER

THE PROTOTYPE Auburn 866 Speedster is assembled and
operating and builder Glenn Pray thinks of his creation
as more than just another entrant in the growing field of
replicars. He bills the 866 as a modernized version of the 851
Auburn Speedster.

Pray has grounds for the claim. He owns Auburn-Cord-
Duesenberg Co., and production by the same firm of the
original speedster and its successor gives the 866 a legitimacy
of ancestry denied most of its rivals.

The 866 is a compromise; standard sedan components fitted with a polyester reproduction of the Gordon Buehrig-
designed 851 body. But then, Buehrig's design was something
of a compromise. The 851 was a combination of standard
Auburn running gear and bodies left over from the earlier
Auburn V-12 speedsters.

Base for the 866 is Ford. Pray starts with a Galaxie frame.
The torque boxes are cut out and the side members moved
closer together and stretched to match the 851's 127-in.
wheelbase. A 428-cu-in. Ford V-8 is moved back 25 inches
and mounted on tubular crossmembers. The transmission is
Ford 4-speed, the limited-slip differential and rear axles are
Galaxie. Stock suspension is retained front and rear, the only
change being a 2-in. cut from the front spring coils.

A lot is new, but it doesn't show. During the time he was
planning the Auburn revival, Pray was doing restorations. An
851 came into the shop and Pray and his crew took molds
from all the body parts. They can reproduce the original,
with some slight changes, in 3-layer, reinforced polyester.

The 30-odd body pieces are bonded to each other and to a
framework of steel tubing before the complete body is bolted
to the frame. Smaller wheels, wide-oval Firestone tires, lower
chassis and side members drop the 866 about five inches below the top of the 851. The new frame and crossmembers allow a cockpit bonus. The floor pan is two inches below the
door sills, while the 851 floor was even with the sills. The 866
cockpit is deeper, if not exactly roomier.

The prototype has a curb weight of approximately 3100 lb
compared to the 3850 of the 851. Horsepower is more than
doubled—365 from the Ford to 150 from the supercharged
1936 Auburn 852. Width and length of both models are the
same, 78 and 205 in.

Wherever possible, Pray used hardware from the original
car. The A-C-D purchase brought with it tons of parts. Door
handles, hand brake, grille, hood ornament, even the orna-
ments halves that decorate the rear quarter panels, came
from Pray's parts bins. A foundry in Denver still has the
molds for the windshield frames and will produce chrome-
plated brass replicas as needed.

Pray's plans for manufacturing may hamper the restoration plans of private owners. If a part is to be used on the

866, Pray won't sell it to anybody else. Pray hopes to counter the loss in good will and revenue with body parts. Where he had to revise for the new car, he kept the original molds, too. A-C-D can supply any body part for an 851 or 852. The owner of an Auburn sedan could buy a complete set and build his own semi-original speedster.

The 866 instrument panel is new but blends with the styling of the car. During the design period, Pray talked with Buehrig and was told to get another dashboard. The 851 had the panel from the standard Auburn. The new panel is engine-turned aluminum. Since it is deeply recessed, Pray hopes to meet federal requirements by padding the cockpit edge.

Pray hopes the production cars will meet all the federal safety regulations, given some luck and some legislation. Ford Motor Co. has been very helpful with the prototype and will provide exhaust emission controls, dual brake system and collapsible steering column. Seat belts and outside mirror are

no problem, and the bumpers and signal lights can be set at any height required. Compulsory crash tests would be impossible for a firm the size of A-C-D, but exemption of the smaller manufacturers is being considered by Congress.

AUBURN 866 SPEEDSTER SPECIFICATIONS

Price, FOB Tulsa, Okla...........$8450	Body.......3-layer hand lay-up polyester
Engine...................ohv Ford V-8	Front suspension: Ford Galaxie; independent with shortened A-arms, coil springs, tube shocks, anti-roll bar
Bore x stroke, in.............4.13 x 3.98	
Displacement, cc/cu in........7014/428	
Compression ratio...............10.5:1	Rear suspension: Galaxie; live rear axle with shortened coil springs, tube shocks
Bhp @ rpm.................365 @ 5400	
Torque @ rpm, lb-ft.......420 @ 3200	Wheelbase, in....................127.0
Carburetion.............one Holley 4-V	Track, front & rear...........62.0/62.0
Transmission.......Ford 4-spd manual	Overall length....................205.0
Brakes................Ford Galaxie drum	Width...........................78.0
Wheels...........15x6JK pressed steel	Height..........................61.8
Tires.....Firestone Super Sport H70-15	Frontal area, sq ft................26.8
Steering type..........recirculating ball	Fuel tank capacity, gal.............25
Turns, lock to lock..................5.0	Weight, lb (approx)..............3100
Frame: revised Ford Galaxie (see text)	Acceleration, 0–60 mph, sec (mfr)....6.0
Seating capacity.....................2	Top speed, mph (mfr claim)........135

THE AUBURN 866

Nostalgia for the hardships of the past may account for much of the classic-car boom, and Pray cheerfully admits that "we designed every possible inconvenience back into the car."

The new Auburn is still a 2-place roadster with classic proportions—big on the outside, small on the inside—with side curtains and a top that can be stowed away neatly by two people trained in the intricate drill. The golf bag hatch behind the passenger's door is functional and the long, cavernous trunk has no hatch. The spare tire must be unbolted from its bracket at the far end, dragged forward and hauled over the seatback.

At this stage in the Auburn revival, the story sounds like an echo. Pray was the prime mover in the Cord 8/10 project, which also featured a promising prototype and went into production. Hopefully, this story will have a happy ending. Pray and some backers bought A-C-D and later formed a separate company to produce the Cord. After assembly began, Pray didn't think it was being done the way he had planned. He and his backers made a swap. Pray traded his share of the production company for outright ownership of A-C-D.

Cord production later stopped and the company was declared bankrupt. Another company was formed, assembled a handful of cars with the parts it acquired and is now reported to be redesigning the car. Mention of Pray and the Cord brings knowing snorts but while he was there when the balloon went up, he wasn't there when it burst.

Pray feels the Cord foundered because the backers tried to move too fast and didn't learn how much speed costs until it was too late. He hopes to avoid the Cord's fate by starting slowly. Four 866s have been ordered. Pray has begun building the first two at his original plant in Broken Arrow, Okla. The new cars will be built in lots of two or three, they won't be started until each is sold, and the work force will be 10 men at most. Write him at Auburn-Cord-Duesenberg Co., Box 15520, Tulsa, Okla. 74115, for information. The 866 is priced at an inflexible $8450, there will be no dealers and the buyer's only option is the color of paint and upholstery.

DRIVING
THE AUBURN 866

BECAUSE NO ONE has ever been trusting or foolish enough to lend me an Auburn 851 Speedster, I can't compare the 866 with its predecessor, but the 866 drives the way a classic looks—big, strong and not very wieldy.

The prototype had been driven more than 13,000 miles and had been disassembled, revised and put back together countless times before the day I drove it, but the car still felt big and strong. Hurtling over railroad tracks produced some odd thumps but they were heard rather than felt and there was no trace of the dreaded cowl shake.

The traditional outside exhaust pipes don't herald the traditional supercharger but performance is well above adequate. The 866 will exceed the highway limit in second gear, or idle uphill in fourth. Pray claims 0-60 in six seconds and a top speed of 135 mph. I didn't try it but I believe it.

Suspension and steering are standard Ford, although the lighter body has the effect of stiffening the springs. Ride is firm but pleasant and the car feels stable at turnpike speeds. The non-power steering doesn't require muscle but it takes a heap of twirling, like five turns, to go from full right to full left. Slalom competition is not recommended.

If the torque makes shifting an option, then the clutch cancels the gain. It's brutally stiff, with two inches separating in from out. The seat, too, is a minus. Yr median-sized obt svt was comfortable, but the 6-ft-plus photographer was a press fit. Pray said the clutch ratio will be changed and a smaller seat fitted to the production cars.

Best part of driving the Auburn were the sensations . . . the imposing view from the driver's seat. . .the rumblings from the exhaust . . . and the gawks from the proletariat.

BY NEIL ERICSON

PHOTOS BY NEIL ERICSON & GORDON CHITTENDEN

CORD SPORTSMAN

A new—and possibly better—Cord to delight the eye and heart of the fwd enthusiast

THE PROTOTYPE of the new Cord has been completed, and it represents quite an accomplishment. In a technological sense it marks a significant breakthrough. In the esthetic sense, it is a near miracle. These two statements are not intemperate adulation. The scaled-down version of what must be considered one of the great automobile designs of all time carries a vacuum-formed thermoplastic body. And to take a great design, fiddle with it in a manner that retains the original width, but lower it and shorten it considerably, and realize a new proportion that works—that certainly requires talent.

The new Cord "Sportsman," and actually the name was

Comparison with Porsche shows relative size of 8/10 Cord which is built on 100-in. wheelbase. Original was on 125-in. wb.

CORD

inherited with its looks, for the old Cord convertible coupe was dubbed the "Sportsman," rides on a 100-in. wheelbase, 25 in. shorter than that of its predecessor. Its smaller 13-in. wheels ride farther outboard in a body which remains 71 in. wide, resulting in a wide 64-in. tread. Its height has been lowered from the original 58 in. to a contemporary 53 in. Its overall length has been shortened to 162 in. from an earlier 195.5 in. It would seem that such drastic deviations from the original proportions might produce an oddity. To the contrary, it can be seen from the photographs that such is not the case, and the car retains all of the charm of the old Cord.

Gordon Buehrig, who was responsible for the original design, feels that the new proportions make the car more attractive than the old one. His reaction stems from its more modern wide stance and lower silhouette. Buehrig was the person who suggested producing the new Cord as a scaled-down version of the original, after viewing the proposed

designs for a contemporary model. The availability of the Corvair engine and final drive unit fitted readily into this scheme, and thus the car was made in its present dimensions. Gordon Buehrig initially intended to help with the scaling of the design, but it was felt that a possible conflict of interest could exist—he heads the plastic body investigation group at Ford Motor Company. In the final analysis, he had no part in the actual development of the car.

Glenn Pray, President of the Cord Automobile Company, and Stanley Bromm, who modeled the car, deserve a great deal of the credit for the success of its appearance. Bromm, former chief of modeling on the Mark II Continental project at Ford, now exercises his considerable skill for the Consumer and Industrial Products Division of U.S. Rubber at Mishawaka, Ind. Pray wanted to capture the look of the so-called phaeton rear deck, feeling it to be more pleasing than that on the convertible coupe. He also wanted to include a jump seat in the rear of the new car which would allow carting about little ones. A restored phaeton version of the 810 Cord was sent by Pray to Mishawaka for use as a guide. The decision to use Expanded Royalite, which incidentally was precipitated when a U.S. Rubber representative called Buehrig while Pray was visiting him, was fortunate for the project. It not only

Instrument panel is virtually original.

Going or coming, it looks, but doesn't sound, original.

...ious change from original is use of external pipes on one side only.

Strictly 2-passenger accommodations.

brought in the skill of Stanley Bromm, but the strength and expertise of U.S. Rubber, and the opportunity to pioneer in the production of a vacuum-formed thermoplastic car body.

Expanded Royalite is a material possessing remarkable physical properties. It is a modified acrylonitrile-butadiene-styrene (ABS) plastic and, in the words of U.S. Rubber, is put together in "... a laminate of substrate, core and substrate, with an addition skin added when weatherability is required. The core is a lightweight unicellular material that functions as the separator for the tough substrate layers and contributes to the *high rigidity* by increasing the moment of inertia for the overall laminate. The substrate functions as a stressed skin and, because of the nature of the ABS terpolymer, affords high impact resistance. This laminate is chemically bonded under high heat and pressure. When the laminate is heated to approximately 300°F. as a part of the conventional thermoplastic forming process, a chemical blowing agent causes the core to expand. The resulting 'sandwich,' Expanded Royalite, possesses a combination of qualities found in no other material."

One very pertinent physical attribute of this material is its exceptional impact resistance. This should prove to be quite beneficial in withstanding minor parking clangs which will

dent sheet metal. A 100 ft-lb impact which ruptured 18-gauge steel and penetrated both ¼-in. reinforced polyester and ¾-in. marine grade plywood made only a small dent in a sample of 0.4-in. thick Expanded Royalite laminate. This dent was completely removed by the judicious application of heat from a 500°F. industrial heat gun. Also, upon failure when its limit is finally reached, the laminate does not leave jagged edges nor produce flying fragments.

As used in the new Cord, the Expanded Royalite was formed in a seven-piece female mold. The body shape had been sectioned vertically, eliminating that portion of each side occupied by the doors, and moved together so that the back door cut met the front door cut. After molding, the body was cut in two at this juncture, the underbody was added, and the doors, actually hollow blow moldings, were hung in the resulting openings. This method of vacuum forming a thick laminate does not encourage the use of very sharp peaks on exterior surfaces. Thus the pronounced pointed fender tips, so characteristic of the 810 Cord, were applied epoxy moldings. This sharpness limitation seems to deter the development of bodies in the current Detroit styling idiom. Increased interest in low drag coefficients would put the process squarely in the running, however. Shapes such as those found on the

...touch of authenticity are retracting headlights which on the new Cord are hand-cranked (from inside) open and shut.

CORD

old Testa Rossa Ferrari or the Costin-Lister-Jaguar campaigned recently at Le Mans would lend themselves readily to the process.

A very attractive feature of vacuum-formed bodies from this modified ABS laminate is the low cycle time involved to produce a body. After drawing the heated sheet into a mold, the material needs to be cooled for 10 minutes. This allows a production rate of six bodies per hour from one set of molds. Tooling costs for this type of body construction are substantially lower than those for steel. U.S. Rubber contends that they are in the order of one percent of the cost for conventional sheet metal. This makes low-volume production runs quite feasible.

The chassis of the new Cord is fairly orthodox, and most of the mechanical components can be purchased from dealer stocks. Even the 13-in. wheel discs, which amazingly approximate the original wheels design, are a stock item, though imported. The front suspension, adapted from a popular French fwd car, does not feature centerpoint steering. Instead, a 1.25-in. kingpin offset was found, a compromise which Pray explains was accepted to preclude any tendency for wheel shimmy. Double cardan joints are used at the outboard ends of the half shafts, with standard U-joints at their inner ends.

The prototype uses a 1964 Corvair turbo-supercharged powerplant rated at 150 bhp. A new exhaust manifold was fabricated, and it is shaped to provide an excellent expansion chamber, minimizing the need for a muffler. The exhaust is carried through the outside pipes to a tail pipe, and actually, this car runs unmuffled. The note is quite pleasant, and not at all too loud. Another sound of mixed origin, from the Corvair fan and turbocharger, lends an authentic whine similar to that which emanates from under the hood of an 812-SC Cord. Though it was a bit loud at the time we had a ride in the prototype, this was a result of some missing grommets in the firewall, an unfinished detail in the first car because of the rush to get it completed. We didn't drive it, but wish we had, to see how much of the torque steering effect common to front wheel drive cars could be felt. This phenomenon is not very pronounced in low-powered cars, but needs to be countered by suspension design and selected tire characteristics in higher performance machines.

Many of the parts used on the exterior of the prototype, as well as the instrument panel in the interior, are original Cord pieces. Some will be used on subsequent models, but others will be re-manufactured. This will make possible the use of the latter in restorations of actual Cords. The holding of the basic car width has made the bumpers, for example, applicable to both the old and new models.

Glenn Pray retrieved the prototype from U.S. Rubber, which had been demonstrating it to various automotive groups around Detroit, just in time for the A-C-D meet at Auburn, Indiana.

We asked what, if any, changes would be found on subsequent models, and were told that one desirable revision would be to hinge the hood at the front. The engine, tucked snugly up to the firewall, lacks accessibility in the present configuration. The top, which was not folding on the car when first demonstrated, now can be operated easily with one hand. The second car, presently nearing completion, will be for U.S. Rubber, and will mount a 110-bhp engine with a Powerglide transmission. The third chassis, now underway, will be powered with a 1965 model turbo-supercharged engine with the modifications which raise its rated output to 180 bhp. It will have a 4-speed transmission. The task on hand at Tulsa is to complete the remaining five of the six projected test cars, learning by doing, and to roll as smoothly into production as possible.

All of the development has been done with private capital, but the Cord Automobile Company, of Tulsa, Okla., will have to go public if it is to achieve its projected 10 units per day production. A lot depends upon the financing and organizing of the company to conduct this amount of business. Glenn Pray, associate and Vice President Wayne McKinley, General Manager Chester Fream, and Production Engineer Walter Carlton III have a big job to do. They are not rushing things to meet a predetermined deadline, but are proceeding deliberately. They have the strength of U.S. Rubber on their side, and George Callum, Vice President of the Consumer and Industrial Products Division, will be pushing hard from his end. The market for a novelty car with nostalgic styling seems to exist in our affluent American society. The ingredients for success appear to be within reach, if not at hand. We wish them that final, essential element, without which no project succeeds—lots of luck.

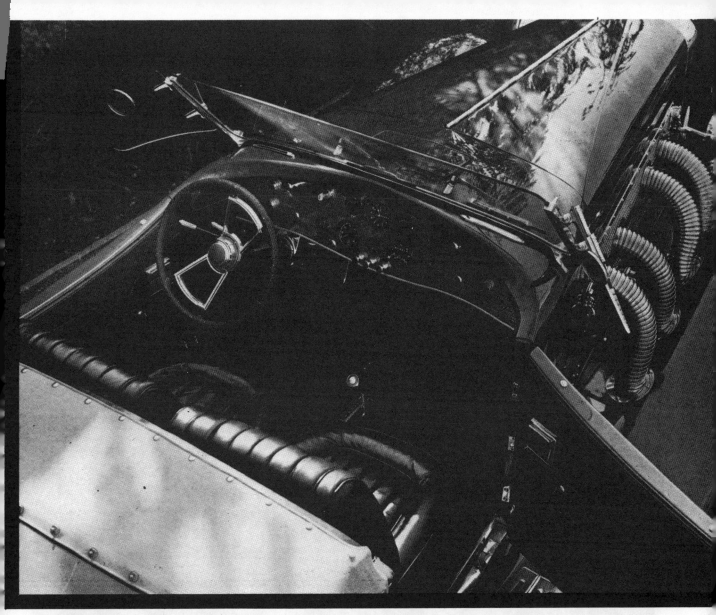

DUESENBERG '71

A new approach to the Replicar

BY JOHN R. BOND

O N DECEMBER 1, 1928, the Duesenberg brothers, Fred and August, announced what must be recorded as the most outstanding automobile ever built in America, if not possibly in the world.

Under the aegis of the firm's new owner, E. L. Cord, they designed, built and sold one of the most remarkable cars of all time. It was, first of all, a huge car, with a wheelbase of 142.5 in. for the standard chassis or 11 in. more for the long-wheelbase option. The straight-8 engine had 420 cu in., not necessarily a record, but two overhead camshafts and four valves per cylinder gave it 265 bhp, more than any other car in the world and more than double the output of any concurrent American car. The original announcement stated that the top speed was 89 mph in second gear, 116 mph in high.

In short, the car, known as the Model J, was an engineering *tour de force* with new and unique features which even today boggle the mind. Of course cost was no object and the basic chassis price, originally set at $8500 complete with fenders, six wire wheels, hood and a cowl section with comprehensive instrumentation, was raised to $9500 in 1931. Think of what that would be in 1971 dollars. And the body was extra and custom built! The average full retail price was between $12,000 and $19,000; a few were reported to have reached $30,000.

About 470 cars were built and nearly half are still extant. Today, 40 years later, a restored Model J will cost you $40,-000 to $60,000, if you can find one for sale.

Now, to go back a bit, while the Big J is the best known example of the classic car collection-inflation mania, other cars have also accelerated in value. In fact even a Model A Ford (an over-restored 2-door Phaeton) is reported to have sold for $4000. An ugly plastic "Glassic" replica on an International Scout chassis will cost you more than that, however.

DUESENBERG '71

With skyrocketing prices it was inevitable that someone would think of building replicars, copies of the now valuable originals with compromises such as a current high-production engine and fiberglass body panels which offer very moderate tooling cost.

The first significant attempt to build such a replicar was by Glenn Pray of Tulsa. He chose the 1936-37 Cord 810 and got the help of Gordon Buehrig, the original designer, and the U.S. Royal Co. (now Uniroyal). The designer took all the original dimensions except width and reduced them to 80 percent of the original. Uniroyal helped with the tooling to promote the use of their sandwich-like plastic material, known as Royalite.

The resultant car, named by *Road & Track* the 8/10 Cord, was successful as a design but the use of a 6-cyl Corvair engine to provide front wheel drive meant rather modest performance as compared with the original. About 100 were built before the firm went belly-up. Another firm bought up the project and sold it to a third firm. Of course the price kept going up and the current Cord replicar has an Ameri-

PHOTOS BY GORDON CHITTENDEN

Driving Impressions

BY RON WAKEFIELD

What an experience for one accustomed to low, compact sports cars of the Seventies to get behind the wheel of such a battleship as the Duesenberg Replica. After all, it is (unlike most replicars) full-size, and that means the bottom of its windshield is as high off the ground as the roof of a Vega and the driver's head is over eight feet behind the front bumper!

Anyway, after heaving the steering wheel its 5½ turns lock-to-lock several times to get the big roadster turned around and headed out of Briggs Cunningham's museum parking lot, I eased out onto public roads with the same trepidation that would have gripped me if I'd been piloting a large truck. The Duesenberg isn't really that big—at 196.1 in. overall it's bumper-and-bumper with the Ferrari 365GT 2+2—but wow, does it seem long!

Extremely touchy power brakes threw me off at first, but once on the road I began to get some confidence about where I could put the car, and the steering (power assistance will be available later) is manageable once you're rolling. The Chrysler engine and Torqueflite transmission behave just as they do in a modern car for normal driving, though Miller has achieved a rather different exhaust note in this car. When the engine reaches 2000 rpm, the high-pitched whir of the Paxton supercharger enters the picture and im-

84

can V-8 engine, rear-wheel drive and revised body contours which the purists consider outright desecration.

At about the same time the 8/10 Cord was getting underway, Brooks Stevens Associates (now called SS Automobiles Inc.) of Milwaukee decided that the famous Mercedes-Benz SSK could be reproduced as a miniature replica. This car, called the Excalibur, has been quite successful (about 500 sold) but it is not an accurate replica and costs more than twice the price of the Corvette from which many of its mechanical components are borrowed. Currently they are about to introduce a diversification program, adding a Bugatti replicar powered by a Chevrolet 6-cyl engine.

There have been and still are a few other replicar projects around including the Ford Glassic mentioned earlier and an Alfa 1750 but none are significant, as yet, except Glenn Pray's latest—his very accurate and full-size Auburn 851 speedster, known as the 866.

But back to the Duesenberg. In 1966 a postwar Duesenberg was announced by a hometown Indianapolis group. The car was designed by Virgil Exner as a modern interpretation of what the Big J might have been. One car was built in Italy (by Ghia) and shown throughout the U.S. The project flopped rather ignominiously—presumably because of lack of adequate financing.

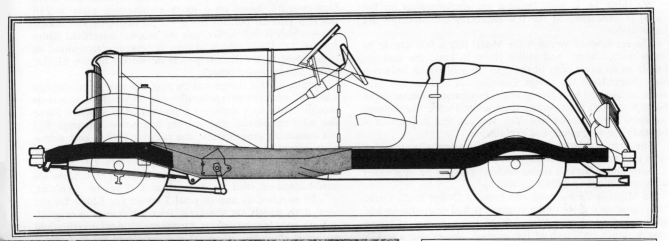

SPECIFICATIONS

	1931	1971
Price, J chassis	$9500	n.a.
SJ chassis	$11,750	n.a.
Speedster	$17,500	$24,500
Wheelbase, in.	125.0	128.0
Track, f/r	58.0	64.0
Tire size	7.00-19	7.50-18
Curb weight, lb.	4400	3600
Engine type	dohc inline 8	ohv V-8
Supercharger maximum pressure, psi	5-8	5-8
Bore x stroke, in.	3.75 x 4.75	4.25 x 3.38
Displacemen.cu in.	420	383
Bhp @ rpm (gross)	320 @ 4200	504 @ 4800
(net)	265 @ 4200	300 @ 4500
Transmission	3-sp manual	4-sp manual or 3-sp automatic
Final Drive ratio	3.78:1	4.10:1
Brakes	drum, 15x3 in.	drum, 12x2.5 in.

parts something similar to the real Duesenberg sound; by 3000 rpm it's developing one psi boost on its way to the maximum five psi at 4800 rpm. (The Paxton supercharger is too small to produce eight psi on the 440 cu. in. engine of the first car.) Mr. Miller didn't want us to do any performance testing so I didn't put a stopwatch on the car, but getting on the throttle hard from a standstill didn't produce anything dramatic—though I expected a lot from a 440 engine, 3600 lb, automatic transmission and final gearing that gives 24 mph per 1000 rpm. At higher road speeds—say 50-60-mph—kicking the throttle brings in 2nd gear again, the supercharger sounds off with a pleasant whine.

Over the gentle undulations of modern asphalt and concrete the big Duesy rides with choppy motions—somewhat more choppy than the original, in fact—but heavier shocks

are on the way and the whole chassis-body assembly seems strong and as well put-together as its superb finish implies. At speed there's the wonderful rush of air to send hair flying, the astonished looks of local gentry in their ordinary modern conveyances and that great outstretched hood that makes an ordinary lane-change into an heroic move—no amount of functional nitpicking could negate the fact that motoring in the 1971 Duesenberg is a marvelous nostalgic experience. For contrast I also took a ride in the original (Gary Cooper's from Cunningham's museum) and must say that the replica is a better car. Bernie Miller says it'll outcorner a Ferrari, and I didn't have the nerve to confront him with reality. I will say that it corners pretty flat. Any enthusiast who yearned for an SJ, never had one and can afford this excellent replica should have one.

DUESENBERG '71

So now we come at last to the "new" 1971 Duesenberg. It can hardly be called a replicar—though it's 98 percent a cold copy of the original, externally.

The instigator of it all is Bernard Miller, a very successful manufacturer of assorted automotive items, both original-equipment and aftermarket, located at 16514 S. Vermont, Gardena, Calif. 90247. When asked how he got into this project all we could get was, "I've always been a car nut, I own three Duesles, the development of the idea has been fun and I think we're on the right track."

We think he is right because the workmanship on the car(s) is excellent and the few necessary compromises are unavoidable.

The car (should we call it the Model K?) is full size, or in other words, huge. And Miller chose to build the first example as an exact copy of the Speedster, of which only two were built. Here the Briggs Cunningham Automotive Museum cooperated by allowing exact, meticulous dimensions to be copied from their perfect restoration. Hence the pictures we show here, side by side. Yes, you can find differences—but they are very minor and explainable.

The first problem with a replicar is, essentially, how far does one go to be accurate—and at what cost? The original J frame and straight-8 engine couldn't possibly be duplicated without millions of dollars for tooling.

So Miller looked around and found a Dodge truck frame that came very close to the original. It had semi-elliptic leaf springs front and rear. With 7.50-18 tires, the top of frame was within a half inch of the original. Wheelbase was 128 in., or only three inches more than the original speedster. (Both speedsters were built on shortened J chassis.) The truck frame was stiffer than the Duesenberg design, could easily be lengthened and offered a wider track—all obvious advantages. Disadvantages were that the front spring horns had to be reworked slightly to taper inwards in plan view, and a special L-shaped plate was necessary to simulate the visual effect under the front fender sweep. This had its virtues, however: it stiffened the frame rails a bit and made it simple to lengthen the wheelbase to original/standard, if required.

The other inevitable compromise was the engine. Since the chassis was basically Chrysler-Dodge they adopted the big Chrysler V-8 engine with a choice of 3-speed automatic or 4-speed manual.

The prototype car shown here has a 440-cu-in. engine with Paxton centrifugal supercharger. Since the complete car with speedster body weighs about 400 lb less than the original *bare* J chassis, they decided to drop to the 383-cu-in. Chrysler engine. At this juncture we must add that this is no ordinary Chrysler engine. The Duesenberg version comes off the special low-production industrial/marine assembly line with all kinds of special features including high-nickel-steel-tipped valves with rotators, hardened crankshafts, heavy-duty bearing inserts, etc. This is not the passenger car engine.

Unfortunately the output claim of 504 bhp is not substantiated even by a 200-bhp net figure at the rear wheels on a chassis dyno. The claimed figure was based on 360 advertised hp plus 40 percent for an 8 psi supercharger boost. Our estimate, based on a lower compression ratio, is 250 net bhp plus 20 percent for a 4-5 psi boost, or 300 honest bhp—which is still well above the original advertised figure for the "J" (265) which in turn is generally recognized as being close to the honest power developed by the SJ (for which 320 hp was claimed).

Despite all this theoretical carping, the new J replicar can and will perform exceptionally well by modern standards though hardly approaching a Camaro Z28 or a Dodge Super Bee with hemi-head. (See driving impressions on page 80.)

Considering other details, the radiator shell is cast aluminum instead of the original stamping. Head and taillights are spun brass to save tooling costs. Fender brackets are cast manganese-bronze instead of channel steel. The fenders are hard-hammered steel (as original) and, if you're interested, will be supplied to any original J owner for $2000 for the four. Body panels are aluminum over ash frames as original.

With very few nitpicking exceptions all workmanship and quality is absolutely impeccable. Considering the fact that a standard 6-cyl Chevrolet of today costs about six times its dollar cost 40 years ago, the 1971 Miller-Duesenberg-Chrysler at double its 1931 price is a bargain at $24,500.

Other body styles will be available at higher prices. Right now the small Duesenberg corner of the main plant is being transferred to a larger facility nearby and the initial batch of 100 cars will be produced during 1971. Ultimately they hope to produce 300 cars per year. The only possible bottleneck will be bodies. If 75 percent order speedsters, no problem. If 75 percent want completely custom bodies, plan on 1972.

Finally, we must admit that even though the price is roughly half that of a secondhand J, there's not too much chance of any appreciation in value. But it sure is a sensational car.

CORD CLASSIC TEST

(*continued from page 38*)

we disliked the feel of the steering and parking was a chore (4 turns, 42-foot circle). The weight distribution of 49/51 unloaded means that considerable power can be applied in a turn without encountering either a front or rear end skid. Unfortunately, applying power means cornering faster; if you let up the rear end slides out, and if you hold the power on, the car ultimately slides broadside. We also felt that there was not enough proportion of weight on the front driving wheels to give the claimed traction advantages in snow or on ice. On wet streets wheel spin was a problem, even in 2nd gear and on the level. Steep grades with wet or loose surfaces would have to be climbed backwards. Performance in general is not as good as, say, the Packard 7-34, but a performance factor of 105.0 cubic feet per ton mile is about average. Obviously the weight of the Cord is a severe handicap in this respect.

The cabriolet convertible body is built by the Limousine Body Company of Kalamazoo, Mich., and shows excellent workmanship throughout. Separation of the instruments into two groups (one at each side) is awkward. The instruments themselves are all of the drum type, which should give easy instant readings. But in practice the markings are too small and the far right group, consisting of gasoline, oil and ammeter gauges, is a nuisance when a passenger is not available for consultation.

In short, the Cord is something of a novelty. It may offer interesting and useful advantages, but it must suffer the trial of awaiting public approval and acceptance. 🔘

THE NEW AUBURN DUAL COWL PHAETON

Glenn Pray has created another "period car"

GLENN PRAY, owner of Auburn-Cord-Duesenberg Co, has designed and built a new car for the enthusiast who wants to relive the magical days of the 1930s. The Auburn Dual Cowl Phaeton Model 874 was previewed by Pray at the A-C-D Owners' Meet in Auburn, Indiana in 1974 and is now in production.

The car is not a replica of any particular model but an interpretation of the Auburn theme by Pray, adapting the best of a number of various cars of the era. It has a 140-inch wheelbase, a completely disappearing convertible top, a 460-cu-in. Lincoln Continental engine, automatic transmission, air conditioning, front disc brakes, power steering and many other standard features. The body is of reinforced polyester and the finish is of hand-rubbed acrylic lacquer with the color to be specified by the purchaser (no metallic colors are offered).

The price is $45,000 FOB Broken Arrow, Oklahoma, and the only extra-cost option is a set of five wire wheels for an additional $1500 if you don't care for the standard steel disc wheels.

Glenn Pray spoke with us on the telephone about his new car and his company. He bought Auburn-Cord-Duesenberg in 1960 and has been operating ever since from a five-acre factory near Tulsa. Pray says the plant used to be a pickle factory and that though its buildings are quite old it suits his purposes quite well. He also mentioned that recent magazine reports (not in R&T) of the sale of the company to a group in Florida and ref-

erences to his having died are, as Mark Twain said, greatly exaggerated. "We've had the doors open every working day for the past 15 years," Pray stated, "and we intend to continue that record."

Pray's ACD Co first gained recognition with the 8/10 Cord in the early 1960s, a few of which we still see here in the southern California area, and that was followed by the Auburn Speedster in 1968. Neither car was a smashing financial success, but Pray is carrying on with his handful of young workers and a dedicated group of Auburn-Cord-Duesenberg enthusiasts who remain quite loyal.

The Auburn Dual Cowl Phaeton will be produced in small numbers, about one per month, and Pray told us the first year's production run is already sold out on the basis of the preview at Auburn, Indiana. It is an elegant car with a number of features often found in vehicles of the 1930s, such as duplicate instrumentation for the rear-seat passengers. A speedometer, tachometer, fuel-level gauge and clock are located in the dashboard behind the rear cowl so that backseat drivers can keep an eye on what's going on. Pray said that he once had a Duesenberg with that feature and his open-cockpit airplanes have it too, so he thought it would be nice in the new Auburn. If you want to be put on the waiting list, write Pray at Auburn-Cord-Duesenberg Co, 122 S. Elm Pl, Broken Arrow, Okla. 74012, or call 918 251-3161.

WEST OF SOUTH BEND, Indiana Route 2 runs through farm country. Corn grows knee-high in three weeks there, and when you step into one of those fields the earth is so rich and soft that you sink to your ankles. Homer W Fitterling owns 2000 acres of that land. His name is hand-painted on his mailbox. Occasionally someone turns into the blacktop drive by that mailbox and asks to see the "old cars." Such casual visitors are politely turned away.

What the idly curious never even glimpse is a 160-car collection that covers six decades of automotive history, from austere 1890s horseless carriages through the modulated flamboyance of 1930s classics to the profligate excesses of a mid-1950s Packard styling exercise. Panhard, Simplex, Rolls-Royce, Stutz, Mercedes, Pierce-Arrow, Lozier, Hispano-Suiza . . . they're all there as are a panoply of others, restored and unrestored, lesser and greater. But Homer Fitterling has focused his efforts on one marque: Duesenberg.

There are 24 Duesenbergs in the Fitterling collection, the largest concentration of Duesenbergs in the world. They sit hub-to-hub along the wall in a 20,000-square-foot converted potato-processing plant along with tons of brass lamps, hundreds of old radios, dozens of 19th-century tools, thousands of emblems and a restoration shop. A dozen years of Duesenberg production is represented: the Model A, Model J and the SJ. There are formal Duesenbergs, touring Duesenbergs, one-off Duesenbergs and sporting Duesenbergs. Five of the two dozen are the nearly forgotten but prophetic Model A;

the remaining nineteen are the fabled J-series cars. They range in condition from pristine show restorations through low-mileage originals to a fenderless hulk desecrated by anonymous hotrodders at a time when Duesenbergs were scrapped for a hundred dollars. One Bohmann & Schwartz "modernization" lay on the bottom of the Pacific Ocean for seven days. Mechanically restored, it now awaits cosmetics. A now-glistening Murphy convertible roadster was found hauling vegetables on an Indiana truck farm. Each car has its story, and Fitterling recalls little details about them in a quiet voice, ambling through the dimly lit warehouse, pausing in front of each one to tell its tale. Nineteen of the cars are complete, five are disassembled for restoration. Parts and bodies are cached in barns around the farm, and Fitterling says he has sufficient stock to restore all the cars. When Homer Fitterling says this, you believe him.

Fitterling began collecting almost a quarter-century ago in a casual, almost accidental way. After flying his plane to Dayton, Ohio to visit friends, he was met at the airport by his weekend hosts in a 1910 Overland touring. They spent the weekend chugging around Dayton in the Overland, and Fitterling enjoyed the experience so much that he asked his friend to find him a car. A few weeks later he was the owner of the Overland. But it was to be a few years before Fitterling discovered Duesenbergs. That happened in 1953 when he found a Willoughby sedan in a Chicago junkyard. A few hundred dollars changed hands and the car was driven back to South Bend. Asked why he bought it, Fitterling says, "It was big,

MR FITTERLING'S DUESENBERGS
He has more of them than anybody else

BY DON FOSTLE

it was impressive and it was made in Indiana." That particular Duesenberg is no longer a part of the collection; it was sold in the late 1950s after restoration. Fitterling estimates that he has owned through the years a total of 27 or 28 of the "Ds" and that "a couple got away."

The period of greatest collecting activity was the decade 1957 through 1967—a time before, in Fitterling's words, "the prices went crazy." [Ed. note: a J phaeton recently sold at the Atlanta auction for a new record high, $205,000!] For a good part of that period an unusual method of locating cars was used. Fitterling owned a large trucking company with offices in 14 cities around the country and "the best way to see the boss was to find him a car." If Fitterling bought the car the enterprising employee would not only get to see the boss but would get a raise. And so the collection grew.

It grew to include the exquisite and supremely rare 1924 Model A roadster shown here. Only 27 Model As were built that year, and though the Model A is almost forgotten today, the Duesenberg brothers Fred and Augie would drive nothing else for personal transportation. The Model A was a subtle and sophisticated "engineer's car." Introduced for the 1920 model year, the "A," as it later came to be known, was powered by a 260-cubic-inch single-overhead-cam straight-8 developing 100 horsepower in its spherical combustion chambers. The typical A weighed only 3300 pounds and abounded in subtleties: aluminum manifolds and firewall, tubular connecting rods, forged steel rocker arms and flywheel, aluminum oil pan, chrome-nickel frame and dozens of other indications of pioneering excellence, not the least of which were the 4-wheel Duesenberg-Lockheed hydraulic brakes.

The Model A was so advanced that the 1924 Indianapolis-winning Duesenberg contained many parts almost identical to their production counterparts except for size. An article in *Motor World* at the time went on for four pages, documenting in drawings and photographs the amazing similarities between the winning 122-cu.-in. race car and its 4½-year-old 260-cu.-in. production sister. But the Duesenberg brothers were not really production oriented; they were master engineers, not canny businessmen. The company threaded its way through lawsuits, hostile stockholder actions, importune government regulations, an economic recession and receivership, managing to produce about 660 cars until E. L. Cord acquired what remained of Duesenberg Automobiles & Motors Company in October of 1926.

Almost immediately Cord announced to the press that it was his intention to build, along with the Duesenbergs, the finest automobile in the world. Cord's pronouncement was neither idle boast nor simple task. The Duesenbergs had done little in the way of forward planning; there were no viable designs for a successor to the Model A. But the car that ultimately emerged at the New York show in December of 1928—called the Model J—bore the indelible imprint of Cord's marketing knowledge, and it was an instantaneous success. Enough orders were taken at the show to occupy the factory for a year of production—at $8500 per chassis (increased to $9500 in mid-1929).

Ninety-five hundred pre-crash dollars bought a magnificently orchestrated metallurgical *tour de force.* Heat-treated aluminum and forged steel abounded on the chassis, which was available in 142½- and 153½-in. wheelbases: dash, instrument board and supports, steering-column brackets, differential housing and cover, pinion housing, torque-tube yoke and brackets, brake backing plates and brake shoes were among the aluminum components. The front axle was a forged I-beam and the rear axle shafts were forged and bored for lightness; the differential's carrier was cast aluminum. The long semi-elliptic springs front and rear had polished leaves, presumably to reduce inter-leaf friction. Suspension control was provided by hydraulic shock absorbers. The 4-wheel brakes were of course hydraulically operated, with 15-in. finned forged steel drums, aluminum brake shoes and power assistance. The frame itself placed great emphasis on rigidity as it was then understood, being constructed of 7/32-in. stock with a maximum depth of 8½ in. on the side rails. It was liberally cross-braced and the engine also acted as a stiffening member.

The engine itself was a fluent translation of racing practice to production design. The 420-cu.-in. (3¾ × 4¾-in. bore & stroke) straight-8 block was cast iron with a removable double-overhead-cam head and four valves per cylinder. Driven by a pair of "silent" 4-row chains, the cams operated directly on silichrome intake and exhaust valves via piston-type followers. The huge Schebler 2-barrel updraft carburetor was fed by a bellows pump from a 26½-gallon tank; fuel and air were delivered to the machined combustion chambers through an aluminum intake manifold. ,Exhaust gases flowed through an immense single manifold into an exhaust pipe of 4¾-in. diameter to a muffler of 54 x 6½ in. and thence to the two 2-in. tailpipes. But the immense cast iron exhaust manifold gave trouble and was quickly changed to two separate castings with dual pipes leading to the muffler.

Ignition was usually Delco-Remy battery and coil, although an occasional later car was fitted with either a magneto or Mallory coil ignition. The pistons were aluminum and carried three rings; connecting rods were also aluminum, though with steel caps. Later rods reverted to the tubular steel section so typical of earlier Duesenberg designs. The forged crankshaft was carried in five main bearings of 2-3/4-in. diameter with bearing widths varying from 1-7/8 to 3-5/16 in. On the crank was a unique vibration damper which consisted of two cylinders 94-percent filled with mercury, bolted to each side of the crank cheek between cylinders 1 and 2. As on the chassis, extensive use was made of aluminum: the flywheel housing, finned oil pan, water pump, timing cover, cam covers and water jacket covers were all light alloy. All aluminum was polished and every visible engine nut and bolt was chromed. Besides being an esthetic delight, the big J engine was claimed to develop

PHOTOS BY THE AUTHOR

This 1924 "A" roadster, above and top left, was one of just 27 built that year. It weighs only 3300 lb and its straight-8 develops 100 bhp.

A hand-formed aluminum top, held in place by only four bolts, gives J-460's Murphy body (left) the look of an early "hardtop convertible."

Homer Fitterling and J-337.

265 bhp at 4200 rpm. This figure was probably reached by experimental engines, but production units were detuned via short-duration cams for better low-speed torque at the expense of some maximum power. These were the engine and chassis that sold out their first year's production at the 1929 show.

Fitterling has one of these early cars (J-124), often distinguishable by their exposed V-shaped Winchester honeycomb radiators and the lack of radiator shutters. It is a Derham-built dual-cowl phaeton on the short wheelbase, and like all Duesenbergs it has its story. The car was originally delivered to the Denver area, where its first owner kept it for about 17 years. After World War II J-124 changed hands and began a process of decay from which it was rescued in the 1960s by a Chicago-area doctor, who was responsible for the restoration. Fitterling traded a 1931 V-16 Cadillac Fleetwood touring for the Derham in 1965 and added it to his already burgeoning collection. Since then J-124 has had only minimum use, spending most of its time in storage to be started and run only twice a year as a part of routine collection maintenance. As far as is known, only one other short-wheelbase Derham Phaeton exists and is in the hands of a California collector.

Among the most popular of Duesenberg body styles was the Murphy convertible roadster, and Fitterling has three of these cars in his collection. J-132 was found on a Michigan City, Indiana farm in 1957. Its owner had been using it as a high-performance means of moving vegetables between his farm and a Chicago produce market. To make the car more suitable to the application, the back of the Derham sedan body had been chopped off and a pickup bed substituted! Fitterling did not purchase J-132 immediately but instead alerted Fort Wayne, Indiana Duesenberg enthusiast Keith Brown to the car's existence. Brown bought J-132 and began restoration, but it was soon apparent that the Derham body was a total loss and another body would have to be found. Fitterling succeeded in finding the needed body in Kansas City, where it had been cast off in a "speedster" conversion of an original car. The Murphy convertible roadster body was transported to Fort Wayne, where Brown mounted it to the chassis. J-132's rear fenders came from still another car, but the total restoration was accomplished with such skill that the car, now owned by Fitterling, was able to achieve 1st in Class at an Auburn-Cord-Duesenberg national meet. Interestingly, J-132's engine and drivetrain have never been touched, despite years of heavy commercial duty.

The Murphy convertible roadsters came with two styles of folding tops. J-132's top sits exposed when folded on the body. By contrast, the top of J-416 disappears into a well behind the front seat, resulting in a much cleaner body line and a better view for occupants of the rumble seat. Fitterling is the second owner of the black roadster, which spent most of its life around Evanston, Illinois before being added to the collection in 1960. He has an uncanny prescience for vehicle value and apparently immense negotiation skills. J-416 illustrates this as well as any of his cars; it was acquired on an even trade for a 1956 Continental Mark II! Since then the dealer who sold Fitterling the car has made attempts to repurchase it.

Although the survival rate for sporting Duesenbergs has been high, the more formal body styles have not fared as well. A much larger percentage of formal cars has been destroyed or altered beyond recognition. The market for used town cars, limousines and formal sedans was not large; as a result prices were low, giving easy access to those who would cannibalize, modify or scrap these elegant vehicles. Though Fitterling has several formal cars in the collection, the most striking is the long-wheelbase Rollston Victoria. It has the appearance of a convertible, but this Victoria has a fixed roof complete with exposed top bows and top liner. The leather interior further enhances the impression of convertibility.

The restoration is an older one, done by a California Oldsmobile dealer, but it has withstood the years quite well. A previous owner was so devoted to this Rollston that he made

Even more convertible-like is J-337, the fixed top of which is covered with beige fabric outside and fitted with exposed bows on the inside.

There is some controversy as to whether this "Gentlemen's Speedster" is actually a proper Duesenberg, but it has always been titled as one.

Left: J-416 Murphy roadster's top folds into a well behind the seat.

Top of J-132, another Murphy roadster, doesn't disappear into well.

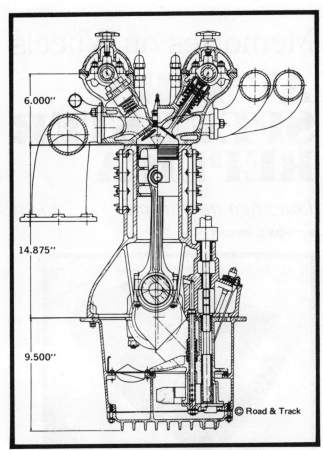

Cross-section of the legendary twincam straight-8 Model J engine.

Its hood side panels, removed, SJ-523 is now Fitterling's "utility car."

J-124 has a Derham dual-cowl phaeton body on the short wheelbase.

payments on it for a period of years before taking possesion. The Rollston's subtle and elegant lines make this totally understandable; it is an entrancing car.

In sharp contrast to the restrained opulence of the J-337 Rollston Victoria is the flamboyance of J-460, a long-wheelbase Murphy coupe with a hand-formed aluminum top held in place by four bolts. J-460 was a one-off creation for George Whittell of Redwood City, California. Mr Whittell, a major stockholder in Matson Steamship Lines, listed his occupation in the Duesenberg factory records as "retired capitalist." He also had an interest in a California Duesenberg dealership, and to boost sales he would purchase new cars. Between 1929 and 1934 he purchased six new Duesenbergs from the dealer, the last of which was an SJ speedster in which Whittell would take his pet lion for rides. Among J-460's other owners was a chorus girl who kept the car for six weeks before selling it to a used-car dealer. Fitterling acquired the car from a Lake Forest, Illinois collector in a package deal which also included two spare J engines and a truckload of Duesenberg parts in 1963. J-460 is completely original and unmodified and shows 12,188 miles on the odometer: even the tires appear to be original equipment. It is one of those strange twists of history that a car once owned by the man who purchased more new Duesenbergs than anyone else is now owned by the man who has more Duesenbergs than anyone else.

As might be expected, Fitterling's collection has its "utility" car, kept prepared for an occasional ride through the Indiana countryside. It is an SJ touring by LeGrande, the "factory" coachbuilder. SJ-523 is notable for its unusually low profile, which in stock form was largely the result of the very short rise of the windshield and top. In the late 1930s the car underwent modifications which included cutting the front fenders and installing a set of 17-in. wheels from a JN. The result of all this is a car that in profile sits very close to the ground and presents a frontal appearance even more aggressive than that of a stock Duesenberg. As a pragmatic concession to the need for occasional engine adjustments Fitterling has removed the side panels of the hood, and the net effect (an anathema to the Duesenberg purist) is one of hairy and *ad hoc* operation readiness. Fitterling's comment about the car, made immediately after a 5000-rpm shift into high, was "If it were the only one we had, it would be good enough." And it is.

Lastly, there is a large white roadster known as the "Gentlemen's Speedster," tantalizingly titled as a Duesenberg and so titled for the last 35 years. Powered by a much-modified Lycoming BB series V-12, the Gentlemen's Speedster was designed by Gordon Buehrig upon a concept developed by Duesenberg President Harold T Ames. There are factory oldtimers who steadfastly maintain that the car was built as a prototype to replace the J series in the waning days of the Cord empire; others, equally certain, say that whatever the car's purpose it was definitely not to be a Duesenberg. Controversies aside, it is a singular and magnificent vehicle of which Fitterling is justifiably proud.

There are 17 other Duesenbergs in the Fitterling collection besides those which have been described. In one sense the choice of particular cars is almost arbitrary, so extensive and wide-ranging is the collection. In the shop area sits a Judkins sedan begun by Fitterling's resident mechanic Frank Knight several years ago. The chassis is completed and the body is in place. It has remained in that state while Fitterling has pursued other activities such as quarter-horse competition and world traveling.

But Fitterling says his interests are once again shifting back to his cars and that he and Knight will restore all the Duesenbergs "now that we're home again." That is a formidable task, but Fitterling is a man who leaves the impression that he accomplishes what he sets out to do. When the restorations are complete—at some indefinite future date—Homer Fitterling will have not simply two dozen Duesenbergs, but two dozen Duesenbergs restored to uniform excellence. It should be something to see.

VISIONS OF ANOTHER era danced through my head as I piloted the California Custom Coach Auburn replica along a winding, tree-lined road on a warm afternoon. The 851 Speedster, built in limited numbers in 1935 and 1936, has always been one of my favorites—massive and imposing but with a spirit that also says, "Go fast!" It was easy to fantasize that I had been transported back to the late Thirties, with World War II still to come and the Depression beginning to wane, money in my pocket, and a lovely lady waiting to be gathered up for a day at the horse races at Del Mar, north of San Diego. Then perhaps an elegant and intimate supper for two in La Jolla, and a late-night drive home on the Coast Highway with a stop at the gambling ships off Long Beach for a throw of the dice, all neatly accompanied by the romantic sounds of Lester Lanin and His Orchestra.

Photographer John Lamm signaling to me to make another pass brought me back to the present and reminded me I was driving a fiberglass replica of the 851, that the money in my pocket might suffice for a Big Mac and my plans for the day were far removed from Del Mar. Oh well, it's all in a day's work. But the Auburn replica is an exciting car that clearly has the capability to evoke such dreams.

The fiberglass body of the replica (called the 876 Speedster) is impressive in quality (¼ in. thick), fit and finish, and the molds were taken from a 1935 Speedster. The attention to detail is

Memories on Wheels
AUBURN SPEEDSTER REPLICA

Long ago and far away . . . today

BY THOS L. BRYANT

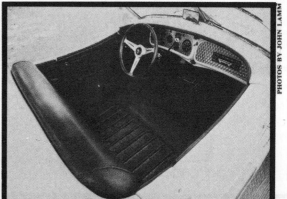

worthy of note, including such nice touches as leather strips laid down between fender and body, the use of chromed brass or stainless steel for all the metal trim, and Connolly leather for upholstery unless the customer specifies otherwise.

The replica Speedster body is mated to a late-model Ford chassis and drivetrain with 400-cu-in. V-8 engine and automatic transmission. The Ford frame rails are lengthened 5.0 in. and beefed up to ensure rigidity. The car I drove had a prototype suspension system that lacked sufficient compliance, resulting in a stiffer than normal ride and lots of body shaking. The Auburn replica measures 205.0 in. in overall length and has a width of 76.0 in., and tips the scales at 3500 lb.

Driving the car is an interesting blend of old and new: The big V-8 provides strong acceleration and the automatic transmission is convenient, of course, while the ride and handling are reminiscent of cars of an earlier era, as are such features as removable side windows, adjustable wind wings and snug-fitting convertible top with its wooden bows. But these are balanced against other modern conveniences such as tilt steering wheel, air conditioning, AM/FM radio with tape player and tinted glass. The replica is large and seems even larger from the driver's seat, with that great expanse of hood stretching to the horizon, offset by the large, bulbous front fenders, and an elevated driving position that gives a commanding view in all directions with the top down. And, as with sports cars, the Auburn replica is best enjoyed with the top down, open to the elements, giving driver and passenger that sense of joyful freedom that comes with open-air motoring.

One factor to be considered in driving the California Custom Coach Auburn replica is high visibility—be prepared to be stared at! No other car in my experience, from the most exotic of the European sports cars to you name it, has ever garnered the amount of attention that this car does. Everyone who sees it, from young kids to grandmothers, takes a second look. In the eyes of elderly ladies, I thought I detected an instantaneous rush of nostalgia and remembrances of dashing young blades of another time. Even "real" old cars don't seem to generate the interest of this one, a tribute to its classic design and probably to its association with playboys and movie stars of the Thirties who seemed to live a fantasy life of opulence amid a decade of depression. Whatever the reasons, this is not a car for those who want to maintain a low profile or slip quietly away for a tête-à-tête.

California Custom Coach (1285 E. Colorado Blvd, Pasadena, Calif. 91106) has been offering the Auburn 876 Speedster in finished and kit forms but the kits are being discontinued as of January 1979. This decision was a painful one, according to the manufacturer, because of the customers who take special delight in building the car themselves, but it was necessary because there have been cases of kits not built to the standards laid down by the company. The completed car, ready to drive, has a price tag of $37,500 for the classic 2-seat model, and CCC has added a 4-seater that sells for $42,500. The 4-seater, while not a true copy of a real model, is nevertheless classic in appearance and offers the convenience of being able to take a couple more people along to enjoy the fun.

Nostalgia in the automotive world has become a sizable movement, with a number of new companies producing cars that look old or classic and yet are not based on any particular model, and other firms producing replicas. Whether or not this is a fad that will pass is anyone's guess, but the fact is there are a number of people willing to spend the money to drive a bit of history. And among the replicas, the California Custom Coach Auburn 876 Speedster is a jewel. ⊗

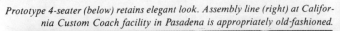

Prototype 4-seater (below) retains elegant look. Assembly line (right) at California Custom Coach facility in Pasadena is appropriately old-fashioned.

Salon
1929 INDY DUESENBERG
One of the fierce breed of Sidewinders

BY JOHN W. BURGESS
Curator, Briggs Cunningham Automotive Museum

PHOTOS BY JOHN LAMM

THE NAME DUESENBERG conjures up visions ranging from ground-shaking monsters to sleek touring cars, formal limousines and elegant town cars. But to the lucky ones who lived in the golden age of racing, nothing made the adrenaline flow through the veins as did the wailing, shrieking sounds of the supercharged high-revving Miller and Duesenberg racing cars.

American speedway racing during the Twenties and early Thirties was conducted under international rules. First were the 2.0-liter or 122-cu.-in. displacement machines, then came the 1.5-liter or 91-cu.-in. racers. Then we had the Depression, a time which practically dictated that automobile racing was far too expensive and so the commonly referred to "junk formula," using stock blocks', was adopted.

The car featured here is from the Briggs Cunningham Automotive Museum (250 E. Baker St, Costa Mesa, Calif. 92626) and was born in late 1929 as a Duesenberg straight-8 91-cu.-in. supercharged machine. However, it never got to race as a 91. Its

first AAA registration card lists it as having a displacement of 142 cu in. through the use of larger cylinder blocks. It was sold (unassembled, I understand) to the famous board track and speedway owner-driver Harry Hartz. The car was driven by a fine driver, Fred Frame, who in turn purchased the car from Hartz. It was later rebuilt for Frame by Myron Stevens, with a new chassis and body to update its performance. Prior to its going to Indianapolis one year, the crankshaft was replaced by a stroked unit to increase its displacement further. I might interject that after the adoption of the junk formula, most of these 91–122-cu.-in. cars fell into the hands of a variety of people, some of whom had good ideas on how to keep them competitive, while others mutilated these technical treasures. (Some powerplants were even cut in half to make midget racing car engines and then discarded!)

The 91-cu.-in. engines were the automotive engineering marvels of their day. In the case of the ones built in Los Angeles by Harry A. Miller and designed by Leo Goossen, they were positively jewel-like in finish and aesthetic appearance, as op-

for painting or plating to enhance its show value. Fred Duesenberg stopped by and Peter explained what he was about to accomplish. Fred stopped him and said, "Will it make it go any faster?" Pete said, "No, it wouldn't." Fred then gave him the curt directive, "Then don't do it."

The car at the Cunningham museum has been brought back to the configuration as last raced by Fred Frame. The original chassis, I believe, is owned by James Haag of New Berlin, Wisconsin. The present chassis is a beautifully done 3-spring unit, using a number of components which Frame was quick to appreciate for their lightness and good design. These include the use of the Bugatti rear axle radius-rod-to-frame brackets, the Bugatti rear end center housing, small and compact, and the large Maserati 4-wheel brakes. Semi-elliptic springs are used on the front, mounted outboard on the frame and snubbed down by the use of single-arm Hartford-type friction disc dampers. As is common with most dirt track cars and some speedway cars of the day, the rear spring is a single Ford transverse unit with double-arm Hartford shock absorbers. A dropped tubular front axle is used with the springs mounted on top. Brakes are hydraulic on all

four wheels, operated by an outside handbrake on the left side of the cockpit. When used on dirt tracks, the front brakes were blocked off. The engine's dry-sump oil reservoir is carried between the front frame members ahead of the radiator. The float-type gauge to check oil level is easily seen behind the radiator shell grille; oil capacity is approximately 4 gal.

The aluminum body is beautifully done, notable for a jog at the firewall section whereby one can open a hinged section and work on the instruments, steering gear and cockpit components. A nicely formed headrest is on a tail section that is sized somewhere between the speedway tails made for the large Indianapolis fuel tanks and the "bobbed" tails used by the half-mile dirt track cars of the period. One noticeable feature of the body is that the right side of the cockpit is built up considerably higher than the left. One great advantage of this design was that when broadsliding a turn on a dirt track, dirt kicked up by the other cars on the outside would not come flying into the cockpit.

The cockpit is a simple affair with the driver straddling the driveshaft and 3-speed Ford gearbox. Throttle is under the right foot, clutch under the left and shift lever in the center. The hand fuel pressure pump is on the right inside the cockpit, and the

posed to the ones from the boards of Fred and brother Augie Duesenberg; their engines were endowed with equal and ofttimes better performance, but lacking the Miller's gleaming, eye-catching qualities. To put it bluntly, Fred made them for go, not for show. A few years ago I was talking with famous Duesenberg driver and Indianapolis winner Peter De Paolo, and he strongly brought this point home. After Peter had won Indianapolis and other great victories on the almost terrifying board tracks, he was preparing some of the car's bits and pieces engine "kill button" is on the 3-spoke steering wheel. A fuel shutoff valve is in the frame channel on the left side, while the fuel tank pressure bleedoff valve is in the frame channel on the right side. A supercharger case drain is operated by a Bowden cable next to the shift lever and driveline. A Bowden cable manual control for the magneto is under the instrument panel next to the hand pump. Instruments consist of tachometer, oil pressure, fuel pressure and water temperature gauges. On the left side of the cowl, aft and above the steering gear, is an opening about 3 in. in diameter. When using the car on the dirt tracks the normal carburetor inlet horn would be removed and a flexible tubing would extend from the carburetor and into the cleaner air of the cockpit.

The engine is a straight-8 with the two cast iron cylinder blocks of four cylinders each, bolted to a 1-piece aluminum crankcase. Each block has four intake and four exhaust ports. Inlet ports are large and oval shaped, exhaust ports are round and slightly smaller. There are two valves per cylinder with intakes slightly larger than exhaust valves. A hemispherical chamber is used and for those who cannot appreciate what little engines these are, the bore is a mere 2.87 in. with a stroke of 3.27 in.

The latter dimension is with the stroker crankshaft which brings the displacement up to a whopping 168.7 cu in. As a comparison, the original crankshaft stroke was 2.75 in. A graceful, tapered 4-port manifold routes water from the top of the blocks to the radiator. Four side ports carry water from the water pump through a tapered manifold to the lower right-hand side of the blocks. Sparkplugs are centrally located.

The aluminum crankcase is a sand casting containing five main bearings. Unlike the Miller barrel-type cases, the Duesenberg units are much wider, thus allowing for the long-stroke crankshaft. Miller crankshaft and crankcase clearances are miniscule, limiting the Millers to larger cylinder blocks as the only means of increasing displacement. Front and rear main bearings use ball bearings with the three center mains being poured babbit, held in place by bronze spiders split in the center and bolted on by four lugs. There are two breather pipes and an inspection plate on the left side of the engine. Solid lugs support

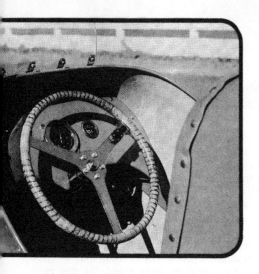

a bracket for the 8-cylinder Bosch magneto on the right-hand side of the case.

On the crankcase, at the center line between the two cylinder blocks, there is an aluminum housing containing a right-angle drive which goes across the engine to the left side at a 1:1 ratio for the supercharger drive. The long magneto and supercharger

driveshafts are parallel with the crankcase and drive from lower gears in the forward-mounted timing geartrain. As noted, all lower aluminum castings are sandcastings and only de-burred, never polished. I took the artistic license to polish only the thin edges of the finned surfaces of the supercharger and intercooler for better photographic definition.

the firewall; it was driven by the two overhead camshafts and this caused considerable problems in the timing because of the inertial forces twisting the camshafts during acceleration and deceleration. The compressor and carburetor were directly above the driver's feet—no place to be if impeller failure occurred. On the 91-cu-in. Millers the supercharger was spur geared to the crankshaft with an inertia slip clutch drive, a vast improvement. I have noted these comparisons to show that real problems existed in supercharger drives. In the case of the Duesenberg, the long driveshaft from the forward geartrain to the right-angled drive acted as a magnificent absorber of the inertia loads similar in action to a smooth acting torsion bar.

The massive 8.0-in. diameter, 20-blade impeller ran at speeds of 30,000 to 40,000 rpm and absorbed close to 50 horsepower. The supercharger's speed step-up was achieved via a planetary drive turning slightly more than five times engine speed. The tip speeds of these huge blades are almost identical to the very small diameter turbos running on today's engines, which often exceed 100,000-plus rpm. The huge compressor case is a typical snail-shape casting with large cooling fins and a centrally located inlet to which a short adapter and a barrel-rotor horizontal Winfield Model D carburetor extend beyond the frame rails. At the bottom of the compressor is a drain valve operated from the cockpit.

The impeller is a beautiful piece of craftsmanship, as is the whole unit. One of the features found only in the Duesenberg supercharger is a needle bearing on the inlet side of the impeller for added strength. The bearing is supported by three struts that not only help brace the rotor but also turn the inlet air from a horizontal flow to a right-angle rotational flow, thereby absorbing the inlet shock on the impeller. This also decreases the compressor load factor, unloads the bearings and has a small effect on temperature rise across the impeller face.

A finned, centrally located supercharger discharge manifold leads up to the horizontal intercooler plenum chamber. The Duesenberg's intercooler is truly a functional piece of technical sculpture, its clever baffling dividing the high air/gas flow equally into four downflow inlet ducts siamesed at the bottom to the

Fred Frame, shown here in the Duesenberg, bought the car from Harry Hartz and had it rebuilt into its present form by Myron Stevens.

The outstanding features of the Duesenberg 122- and 91-cu-in. engines are their supercharger installations. The supercharger is located with its compressor housing parallel to the center line of the engine but driven at right angles to the engine. Because of this feature, they were known as "sidewinders." An advantage of this was the centrally located intake manifolding being symmetrically better for distribution to both cylinder blocks. In contrast, the 122-cu-in. Millers had their supercharger located on

eight engine inlet ports. The downflow ducts are exquisite pieces of work with the inside of each one having nine guide vanes to direct the flow properly all the way to the inlet ports. Care such as this in controlling the gas flow is seldom seen today.

The use of the intercooler helped the efficiency of the supercharger as the compressed air/gas coming off the tip of the supercharger gets hot and expands rapidly, dropping the volumetric capacity of the inlet charge. This particular intercooler is

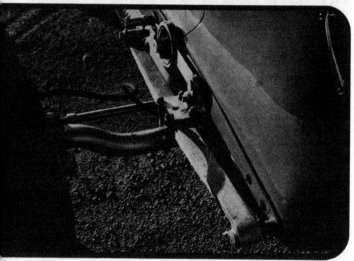

the smaller of the two that were used on this engine. The first ones were almost double in height and hung out in the airstream for maximum cooling. This worked fine except it blocked the circle track driver from closely observing his left front wheel and also resulted in uncomfortable aerodynamic buffeting at high speeds. The small intercooler fits snuggly under the engine hood and there is a row of louvers which brings air across its fins. The whole engine area in this car, as well as the body, is underpanned, a really beautiful job which results in all the air coming through the radiator and louvers passing directly over the areas where it is most needed.

The supercharger/intercooler system was designed by Dr Sanford Moss and only a few top mechanics were entrusted with the careful assembly work that was necessary. And just as a watchmaker left his hallmark in the case, so did the men who assembled these units. In the Duesenberg diffuser section are inscribed three names, one of them Fred Frame's.

Noise was one of the most exciting and impressive characteristics of these sidewinders. When nearing a speedway or board track, one could hear the superchargers 1½ miles away. First there was a wailing sound as the engine changed rpm on the turns, growing into a shriek at full revs at the end of the straightaway. Then, as the car passed, the beautiful exhaust note of a straight-8 engine running somewhere around 6500 rpm, with some as high as 7500. One has to remember this was more than 50 years ago and the speeds for 91-122-inchers were not too bad either, even by today's standards. For instance, consider this: 285 bhp at 8100 rpm with a 30-psi boost and a straightaway speed of 164 mph at Muroc Lake ... a qualifying speed on the 1.5-mile Amatol banked board track at Atlantic City, New Jersey of 147.7 mph ... and Leon Duray's 148.1 mph on the 2-mile, banked and brushed concrete track at the Packard proving grounds in Michigan.

Yes, these were machines which set the pace for performance, technical know-how and aesthetic qualities for years to come.

Racing cars were designed to be winners, or else why bother?

By the time the car was built it was a 100:1 bet that it had already deviated from the drawings. The next phase was testing—again, another 100:1 bet that there would be changes. Each race proved the design, and the worth of its brave driver. Even if the car proved to be a winner, updating had to continue until such time as the car was retired. When restoring such a vehicle, unlike a production car, one must ask oneself: "To which race do I want to restore this machine?"

I recall all too vividly this machine in its original form. It was a real terror on the dirt tracks and the Fred Frame-Billy Winn duels on the eastern fairgrounds circuit tracks are legendary. Frame was a race driver's race driver, the epitome of the professional of the Twenties and Thirties, who rose to fame from the dangerous dirt tracks. Fred won Indianapolis in a Miller in 1932 and made 2nd place in 1931 in the Duesenberg. On the cornfield dirt tracks where most drivers were ham-fisted, Fred was deceptively smooth, a real asset, especially when running a small-displacement engine. When you are very young and starting out as a racing driver, you are what is known in the profession as "lead-footed and balloon-brained." I found this by going way over my head into a turn with the thought that I could beat or at least hold the Duesenberg throughout the turn. Fred was behind me going in, but almost at the apex I was sideways—flat-out—and hoping I was going to make it. Fred got the Duesie underneath me and at this critical moment as I looked across, Fred put both hands up to his goggles. I instantly thought, "What is happening to him and who in hell is steering the car?" A good handling car on dirt, once it has been set up, will go through in a beautiful line by just using the throttle. The reason I couldn't see was because of the high right-hand side on the cockpit. Fred had stuck his knee against the steering wheel holding it just long enough to reach for his goggles, giving me the feeling that he was in trouble and going to drift out, taking you-know-who out through that 2-rail fence with him. I backed off in a hurry, and Fred went by in a hurry. After the event I told Fred, "You surer than hell scared the daylights out of me in the middle of the first turn." He grinned and said, "It works on you young guys every time." Talk about being had.

It is quite a thrill to drive a car of this nature, not just for the nostalgia of reliving old memories but evaluating it as a piece of automotive engineering at its finest. There are several things one has to adjust to, the number one item being tires and tire sizes. Mother, bless her soul, goes to the market with a bigger patch of rubber on the ground on a single tire than these older cars had on all four. This obviously means that the Duesenberg driver had to be sensitive to the car's needs. Being a fairly stiffly sprung automobile with solid front and rear axles, the message of what's happening is quickly transmitted through the seat of the pants. This car, with spool-axle-locked rear end, is typically a strong oversteerer, but also very definite in its reaction to steering and power inputs. Balance seems quite good, varying, of course, to the degree of fuel tank size and fuel load with the large tank being for Indianapolis, the smaller one for dirt tracks. Steering is relatively heavy by today's standards but this is good, as it does temper one's tendency to overdo things.

We have run this car only on the paved museum parking lot, a 2½-acre area. Driving fast cars in an area such as this is similar to playing a slide trombone in a telephone booth—it keeps one alert. One has to drive rather smoothly on the pavement turns and accelerate out on the very short chutes. The blower doesn't really come on until you get almost too close to the end. A centrifugal supercharger output curve is rather low at low rpm but at 4000-plus it starts up almost in a vertical line. It's like getting a terrific upholstery-flattening push. I've wondered for close to half a century what it would be like to drive this car; however, it's ironic that running it at the car's (or is it your?) potential is similar to life: By the time you are in a position to do a lot of things you've always wanted to do, you're too old to do them. I guess the thoughts of winding it up with its supercharger screaming like a banshee and throwing it sideways into a dirt track turn are now just a Walter Mitty dream—but what a dream ...

Salon

◆ 1932 ◆
DUESENBERG
MODEL J SPEEDSTER

The best of American chassis clothed in fashionably French style

BY DEAN BATCHELOR
PHOTOS BY JOHN LAMM

THE HEADLINE IN *MoToR* magazine for December 1928 read "265 Horse Power ... 116 Miles Per Hour ... Duesenberg Announces an Extraordinary Car with Chassis Priced at $8,500." In its December 1928 issue, *Automobile Topics* said "New Duesenberg of the 'Super' Type. Wheelbase length is 153½ Inches—265 Horsepower Engine—Lavishly Built and Unusually Well Designed."

Automobile Topics went on to say: "The car that Fred S. Duesenberg has always wanted to build is out at last, and will have its premier showing at the Salon in New York next week. When E.L. Cord, President of the Auburn Automobile Co, purchased Duesenberg Motors in 1926, he announced it as his purpose to build, with Fred Duesenberg's assistance, the world's finest automobile. It is this car, spectacular, big and fast, which is now being disclosed."

After an introduction like that a car would have to be outstanding to live up to the billing. Big, powerful cars that displayed the opulence of their owners were nothing new; Rolls-Royce, Isotta-Fraschini, Minerva, Hispano-Suiza, Mercedes-Benz, Stutz, Packard. Lincoln and Cadillac had been building them for years.

The Model J Duesenberg was more powerful (more than double the power of its nearest domestic competitor, the 112-horsepower Chrysler Imperial 80), faster, more expensive and visually more impressive than any of its contemporaries. It was unique in being the only American production car to have an engine with twin overhead camshafts—it was the one car that had an engine compartment as beautiful as the car's exterior, and just as well finished.

The first public appearance of the new Duesenberg was in the 1929 New York Automobile Salon held at the Commodore Hotel in December 1928. The press, particularly the automotive writers, loved the car but lavished most of their praise on the engine—a straight-8 with 420 cu in. (6885 cc) and putting out its maximum horsepower at 4200 rpm.

Duesenberg cars were named after their designers, Fred and August Duesenberg, two brothers who had emigrated from their native Germany 50 years earlier, but credit (as the real creator of the Duesenberg) has to go to Errett Lobban Cord for his determination to build the finest car in the world.

Cord, who had been a successful automobile salesman and later a dealer in Chicago, bought the ailing Auburn Automobile Company in 1924 and quickly turned it into a profitable manufacturer of moderately priced cars. Two years later Cord bought Duesenberg and about the same time purchased the Lycoming Engine Company, which would build engines for the new cars.

Three Duesenbergs were on display at that New York Automobile Salon, with bodywork by Le Baron, Murphy and Holbrook, and none of the three was finished by show time. All three cars were sold during the Salon, with the understanding that the deliveries would be made once the cars were finished and tested. Deliveries started in the spring of 1929.

None of the three Duesenbergs on display had the name on the car; it was Cord's idea that his cars were so good they didn't need identification. But by the time they got into production there was a Duesenberg crest on the radiator shell and on the firewall in the engine compartment.

Only the chassis, which sold for $8500 in 1929, was built by Duesenberg. Customers ordered bodies for their cars from catalogs with illustrations of the many types of coachwork available from Bohman & Schwartz, Brunn, Derham, Dietrich, Judkins, Le Baron, Locke, Rollston, Murphy, Walker or Weymann.

A complete Duesenberg J delivered to the customer in 1929 cost from about $11,500 to around $13,000. When the supercharged SJ was introduced in 1932, its chassis price was $11,750 and the delivered price went to as much as $20,000 for the Buehrig-designed, Rollston-built Arlington sedan, which came to be called the "Twenty Grand."

For the price of a 1984 Volkswagen Scirocco, the Duesenberg customer of 1929–1930 got the biggest, most powerful, fastest and—depending on choice of bodywork—one of the most beautiful cars on the road.

The big J was a match for anything on the road in any respect. Two wheelbase lengths were used: 142.5 and 153.5 in. The main difference in the two was the length of the frame, driveshaft, exhaust system and brake lines. Five (or less) passenger bodies were built on the short wheelbase, while the longer one comfortably accommodated a body large enough for seven passengers, but this practice wasn't always followed.

The Duesenberg's ladder-type frame is a massive structure with ⁵⁄₃₂-in. thick side channels, 8½-in. deep with 2¾-in. flanges, connected into a strong and rigid unit by six tubular crossmembers, the largest being a 4½-in. square, and the smallest a 2¼-in. round tube. A pair of 2-in. round alloy steel castings, 2 ft long, run diagonally from the second crossmember rearward to the frame side rails. These braces give the front of the frame the stiffness that Fred Duesenberg thought necessary to help prevent front wheel "tramp" and, at the same time, serve as front engine mounts.

The front axle, a drop-forged I-beam, and the semi-floating hypoid rear axle are attached to the frame by 2½-in.-wide semi-elliptic springs, 41 in. long in front and 62 in. long at the rear.

The polished spring leaves are encased in dirt-proof covers. Shock absorbers are Lovejoy double-acting hydraulic units.

A car with the mass of a Duesenberg (a J Sport Phaeton weighed about 5270 lb and a Formal Limousine could top 7000 lb), and its top speed potential (in 1929 Duesenberg literature claimed 89 mph in 2nd and 116 mph in top gear), should have the best brakes available, and the Duesenberg did—within the parameters of automotive knowledge at the time.

Duesenberg's 4-wheel hydraulic brakes had forged steel drums 15 in. in diameter and 3 in. wide, and were finned for added drum rigidity and cooling. Two brake shoes, made of cast aluminum, were used in each drum, but the parking brake was a 3-in.-wide, 8-in.-diameter drum with external contracting shoes, mounted on the driveshaft just behind the transmission.

Six 19-in.-diameter, 6-in.-wide wire wheels were furnished with each chassis in 1929. The SJ, when it came out in 1932, was equipped with 17-in. wheels and buyers then had a choice of either size for either model.

The Model J's Lycoming-built engine followed racing car practice by having twin overhead camshafts, and there are two intake and two exhaust valves per cylinder. The cam lobes act on cup-type followers between the cam and valve stems. Camshaft drive is by a 2-in.-wide silent chain driven off an idler that, in turn, is driven by a similar chain from the massive crankshaft, which runs in five main bearings.

The crank is statically and dynamically balanced, and a unique system developed by Fred Duesenberg was incorporated to ensure further smoothness. This balance mechanism, which is mounted on the crank cheeks between numbers one and two cylinders, employs two chambers, each of which is approximately 2 in. in diameter and 3¼ in. long, containing 16 oz. of mercury—occupying only 94 percent of the chamber. Because mercury "seeks its own level" more quickly than any other known element, any periodic vibration in the shaft is quickly damped by the movement of the mercury within the cartridges.

A single sparkplug per cylinder is located at the top center of the combustion chamber, and special effort is made to cool the engine by having water jackets the full length of the piston travel, and almost full length of both valve stems and sparkplug bosses. Oil is fed under pressure to all main, connecting rod and camshaft bearings, and all accessory drives, after being filtered twice—once by a normal sediment trap before entering the oil pump, and then by a Purolator filter between the pump and the engine.

All the working parts of a Duesenberg are as beautiful as they are sturdy and powerful. A great deal of thought and effort went

into the appearance and finish of every part because Cord and Duesenberg wanted it done that way. Fred Duesenberg always specified the material he thought best for a given application and the result was that a considerable amount of aluminum was used. This had a side benefit of lightening the car somewhat. Corners weren't cut to save money.

All aluminum parts are polished, and other parts are either enameled or plated. Every Duesenberg J and SJ engine built by Lycoming (about 480 in all) was enameled bright green with polished aluminum valve covers. They are gorgeous power-plants but if the body color contrasts too much, the view with the hood open can be disturbing.

A Duesenberg's beauty isn't limited to the mechanical components. During the nine years in which the Duesenberg J and SJ were built, the marque displayed some of the best bodywork in the world, in both appearance and craftsmanship. One of the reasons for the marvelous coachwork was the company philosophy, carried out by chief designer Gordon Buehrig, which dictated that the coachbuilder be furnished a chassis that included the fenders and running boards, bumpers, six wire wheels and tires, headlights and taillights, radiator, grille and hood. Starting with these components, the custom body included everything behind the cowl and above the frame, which result in a unique appearance, but with a family resemblance to other Duesenbergs. Some Duesenberg J and SJs appeared with non-standard grilles, fenders and hood and, with few exceptions, they didn't look as good as those that had the Duesenberg look.

One of E.L. Cord's goals had been to invade the European market and he was aided in this by E.Z. Sadovich who established a sales agency in Paris called Motor de Luxe. Approximately two dozen J and SJ chassis went to Sadovich, and he used the best of the Continental coachbuilders to clothe them in exquisite and often flamboyant shapes. Among the body suppliers to Motor de Luxe were Hibbard & Darrin (later Fernandez & Darrin), Letourneur et Marchand, Franay, Saoutchik, Kellner, Graber, Castagna and Joseph Figoni (later Figoni et Falaschi).

Figoni, it seems, built only two bodies on the Duesenberg J—a convertible Victoria (which was a re-body of a Judkins limousine) and the French Speedster shown here. In typical Duesenberg fashion this creation has stock hood, grille, bumpers and lights, but it has fenders that are unique, and no running boards, this function being cared for by elliptical step-plates finished in red and chrome. Chassis furnished to European coachbuilders included the radiator shell, the hood and the six wire wheels, but not the fenders, running boards and bumpers. This left a great deal more of the design open to the

coachbuilder and it helps explain the configuration of the French Speedster.

The car has undergone a considerable metamorphosis since it was built in 1932. As originally delivered, it had the typical J hood-sides with curved louvers and a 2-tone blue paint scheme similar to the red-and-black combination that it has today. After World War II it was seen with entirely different taillights and in a single color.

At some time in recent years a replica supercharger was added and the exhaust routed through outside pipes (covered with chrome-plated flex tubing) on the right side of the hood as seen on SJs. The original-style Duesenberg head and taillights now on the car replaced the French lights originally installed, and the car now sports a pair of replica Pilot Ray driving lights in front of the radiator.

The car has also had at least two different windshields (one tall and one low), with and without windshield wipers, and several upholstery jobs, one of which was tan pigskin. The basic body form and the short fenders, which are reminiscent of Thirties aircraft wheel "pants," seem to have remained pretty much as originally built.

The overall form and design are very pleasing, with well integrated shapes, but some of the detailing—particularly the 2-tone paint division—is disturbing. The sweeping line coming off the hood top and down the body side ends abruptly at the lower rear corner of the door as though the designer didn't know what to do with it (Buehrig's treatment of the side of the Weymann-bodied SJ Speedster is far better), and the red of the cockpit area that sweeps into a point at the back top of the body is less than satisfactory, ending as it does in a "pointless" point. The car is spectacular as is, but could make a far more cohesive design statement with a better paint scheme.

When the Speedster was completed by Figoni, Sadovich entered it in the Paris-Nice Rally, where it finished 17th. The Rally wasn't the real event that attracted Sadovich, however, it was the Concours d' Elegance in Monte Carlo immediately following the Rally that interested him. Showing new models in a Concours was excellent exposure for such a company. Sadovich later sold the car to Antonio Chopitea, a Peruvian playboy, who later entered it in the Concours at Cannes, France, where it took first place.

This French Speedster is currently part of the magnificent Blackhawk Collection in San Ramon, California. A marvelous amalgam of American chassis and French coachwork, it will be on display in the 1932 Auto Show section of Auto Expo '84 at the Los Angeles Convention Center from May 19–28, 1984. ◉